One More
Child

By Felice Gerwitz

Media Angels®, Inc.

One More Child

Published by Media Angels® Inc.
Fort Myers, Florida 33912
www.MediaAngels.com

© 2018 by Felice Gerwitz
ISBN 978-1-931941-29-7

All rights reserved. No part of this publication may be reproduced, stored in a retrieval system or transmitted in any form by any means—electronic, mechanical, photocopy, recording, or otherwise—without prior permission of the publisher, except as provided by U.S. copyright law.

Unless otherwise noted, Scripture texts in this work are taken from the *New American Bible, revised edition* © 2010, 1991, 1986, 1970 Confraternity of Christian Doctrine, Washington, D.C. and are used by permission of the copyright owner. All Rights Reserved. No part of the New American Bible may be reproduced in any form without permission in writing from the copyright owner.

Printed in the United States of America
Cover and Layout: Bob Ahrens
Editors: Janice Neyer and Mary Jo Tate

This book is dedicated to my husband, Jeff.
Thank you for asking me to marry you
and for all the wonderful years.

To Neal and Christina, children of my younger years,
and to Nicholas, Anne, and Michael,
the children of my Elizabethan age.
You have all made my life special.

Published in 2018 on the 50th Anniversary of
Humanae Vitae

CONTENTS

Preface vii

Introduction xi

CHAPTER 1 Life Begins 1

CHAPTER 2 Life Circumstances 11

CHAPTER 3 Intelletual Information 23

CHAPTER 4 Reality of Life 31

CHAPTER 5 Happily Ever After 37

CHAPTER 6 Devastating News 43

CHAPTER 7 Coming Home 53

CHAPTER 8 Life With Kids 69

CHAPTER 9 Unexpected Blessings 83

About the Author 93

One More Child

Preface

Does "happily ever after" happen in real life, or is it merely a fairy tale perpetuated by the media? This is a question each of us needs to answer. Happiness comes in all shapes and sizes. Maybe you've asked yourself the following questions: What is the plan for my life? What will I do for a profession? Where will I live? Whom will I marry? How many children will I have? If you think about them seriously, the answers to these questions are fluid. As we grow and mature, our ideas often change. We can hope to live a happily-ever-after type of life that meets our goals, ideals, and dreams, but life has a way of shaking our convictions. Obviously, only God knows the future.

For many people, happiness depends on our family life. I believe that children are gifted to us by God. Many people decide to limit this gift due to a preconceived notion of how they wish to live their lives. God has a wonderful plan, and many of the struggles against His plan are caused by our free-will choices. Emotional ups and downs in our lives are often a direct cause of our decisions. Sure, some things are totally out of our control, but the way we react to these events reveals much about our true selves. Stopping to analyze our state of mind or, more importantly, our reactions to uncontrollable life events will show us where we are in our walk with God.

I don't have all the answers. I have dragged my feet for years trying not to write this book. I've had misgivings because discussing birth control or other permanent solutions is a touchy subject. Openness to God's plan for love and life is a subject about which even the most even-tempered people vehemently disagree. How dare I discuss the idea of being open to having children—especially to having more children? No one likes advice about such a personal decision, no matter how well-meaning. Our world is inhospitable not only to children but also to the idea of motherhood. Over the years, my own views of authentic womanhood and motherhood have changed, and I'm still learning and growing in my walk with God.

I'm writing this book to put to rest the persistent and nagging sense that some of you may need to hear what I must say. Or perhaps, like me, you have misgivings about limiting the number of children in your life. I've learned that many moms and dads are hurting and confused. They feel pressure from well-meaning family and friends, as well as societal viewpoints, all claiming to know what is best when it comes to family size. They hear questions such as "Of course you are done by now?" or "Really? Another baby?" or "Do you know what causes that?" or "Are you trying for your own baseball team?" or in my case, "How old are you?"

The answers to my personal decisions involving these questions and more are explored in this book. For a public speaker, podcaster, and author, I'm an anomaly. I'm actually a private and shy person—but no one seems to believe that about me! The very fact that I'd reveal a portion of my life—a tragic mistake that no one needs to know about—to all of you is an act of obedience to the God I serve.

Perhaps I couldn't share this story if it didn't have a happy ending. In fact, this wonderful outcome could only happen by the grace of God's merciful and forgiving love for me. And the best news? God's answers to our prayers are so much better than anything we can imagine—and believe me, I have an amazing imagination! God has an abundance of grace that He is happy to share with all of you as well.

One More Child

Introduction

It has taken me over five years to write my story because the timing did not seem right, or so I told myself. As I think back over the events, time seems to stand still and I clearly see the day when God made it clear that I needed to share my story with you.

It isn't every day that I think I hear God as I'm travelling seventy-five miles per hour on the interstate with my family. It happened suddenly without any warning, and it was so real that I wanted to turn around to look behind me. I thought, "He's right there!" Before you think I'm certifiable, let me explain.

We were travelling to a theme park about two hours from home. As we drove toward Tampa, we passed a billboard advertising the doctor who had performed our vasectomy reversal. This doctor is striking, and his face is plastered on the billboard along with the word *Vasectomy* for the entire world to see. Seeing the billboard arouses anger inside of me each time I see it because it brings back mixed feelings.

My husband and I both knew that we had made a tragic mistake. At first we realized it individually, and then Jeff was bold enough to share with me his regret for having a vasectomy. That was an important turning point for us individually, for our faith, for our marriage, and for our future children, if we had any more. You see, this doctor hadn't wanted to perform Jeff's reversal surgery, although he was very skilled at the procedure. We already had a boy and a girl, so he couldn't imagine us wanting more children. Also, we had waited twelve years before seeking a reversal. The doctor had given Jeff so many dire warnings the first time we went for a consultation that we left without scheduling the surgery. It had taken another full year of prayer and discussion before we attempted scheduling this surgery again, and then another presurgery consultation had been required. This time, however, we had both been convinced that this was something the Lord wanted us to do, so Jeff had the surgery.

After reading the words on the billboard for the umpteenth time, I heard the Lord speak: "How long will you continue to allow Me to be mocked?"

What?! I wanted to turn around because the voice was so real, and I knew whose voice it was. I had no doubt! The voice and the message were strong and convicting. I knew exactly what He meant in an instant of grace. So what was I supposed to do with this knowledge? Start boycotting the doctor? No, he does good work when he performs reversals. So what then?

I prayed. Slowly, I realized that I should tell my story, and I didn't like it. Yet I knew in my heart it was what I needed to do. I needed to make my story public. Yes, I was already an author, but this wasn't the type of thing I write. In fact, as a consultant, I often advise aspiring authors against writing autobiographies or memoirs because few people want to read them except when they are about famous people.

So why am I writing a memoir almost five years after I heard the voice? Because God's timing is not my timing. And many things needed to fall into place for this book to happen. In fact, as I was mulling over the idea of writing a book and arguing in my mind with the Lord that He had the wrong person, it hit me that I had the perfect excuse! I prayed, "Lord, you know that authors need a platform. How can I invest money in publishing this book if I have nowhere to speak and tell people my story?" There—that was done! I thought I was off the hook until several days later I received a phone call from a ministry where I volunteer, asking me to give my testimony!

At that point I had been involved with this ministry for over ten years but had never been asked to speak. Why were they asking now? No one knew about my pleading with the Lord to be relieved of this perceived mission . . . but He knew. Being asked to speak was no coincidence. I knew that the Lord had provided a platform for the book and that I would be His hands and feet in this, no matter what the cost.

As you read my story, please understand that I'm not pointing any fingers or saying that if you do such-and-such, you are going to hell. I am not the type of person to condemn. Only God knows each of our hearts and motivations. In addition, this isn't the story of a perfect life with a formula for you to follow so that you will be singing with the angels in heaven alongside me. However, this book does have a very strong and important message: God has a beautiful plan for authentic womanhood for each of us, married or unmarried. And this plan runs counter to the secular view of womanhood that has duped many of us far too long.

I wrote *One More Child* in the hope that you too will feel the call to be open to new life. To emphasize that, I've included information about the nine months of the growth of a baby in the womb at the beginning of each chapter, with accompanying Scripture verses.

In reading this book, you will see how, with the grace of God, I answered the question that God asked me, "How long will you allow Me to be mocked?" This book explains my answer: "Not one second longer, Lord. Not one more second!"

Chapter 1
Life Begins

Before I formed you in the womb I knew you, before you were born I dedicated you, a prophet to the nations I appoint you.
— Jeremiah 1:5

Month One

The miracle of life begins after fertilization. The dividing cells organize themselves in groups, a plan that God, the creator, put into the essence of what it means to be human.

In a few weeks, the heartbeat can be heard, often before the mother knows she is pregnant. At three weeks, the baby has developed all the necessary genetic material, and the sex is already determined.

****

We don't get to choose our parents—something my kids probably lament in private! My parents were wonderful, and I realize that more with every passing year since their deaths. Both were born in Sicily, and both were uneducated by the world's benchmarks. My mother finished the sixth grade in Palermo, and my father completed the fifth grade on the coast of Messina. However, both were financially successful due to determination, hard work, and entrepreneurship. My grandmother who lived with us demonstrated unfailing faith and strength. I never imagined my friends' families being different from mine, but I soon learned I was mistaken.

Being born in a family of Italian immigrants had its advantages and disadvantages. On the plus side, there was an abundance and variety of food. We ate well! In our family, there are big distinctions among linguine, spaghetti, and fettuccine; in fact, we had arguments over when to use each type of pasta. On the flip side, being an American-born kid in an Italian family of immigrants created a lot of pressure to succeed. My mother, who came to America at age twelve, never let me forget that this country was a wonderful land of opportunity.

Although my parents were born in Italy, my mother's first marriage was arranged here in the United States. She waited until she was almost thirty years old because her sisters had to marry first, as is custom. She and her sisters worked in the garment district in New York City. She always credited the union with the fact that she had fabulous hospital care when I was born at Mt. Sinai Hospital. The arranged marriage was very short lived, and my biological father left right after I was born. The circumstances were never discussed.

Despite this, I had a great childhood surrounded by love. My grandmother and my Uncle Sal, who was deaf, lived with my mom and me. I was literally raised at my grandmother's feet. While I helped her wrap yarn into balls for her knitting, she told me stories about the Bible: Adam and Eve, Noah, Abraham, Moses, Mary and Joseph, Jesus, and of course the Apostles. I felt that I knew these people and they were my friends. Of course, the stories of the saints were also second nature. One of my favorites was Padre Pio, now Saint Pio. I loved hearing about his heroic virtues.

In addition, I was surrounded by a big family; I grew up with my cousins, aunts and uncles. Everyone was named Rose, Mary, or Josephine or Anthony, Angelo, Salvatore, or Joseph—except for me. I was named after my maternal grandfather, who died before I was born, so not only was I stuck with the name *Felice*, but it was the male version! It was hard to explain to my teachers when they called me Felicia or Felicity.

When the movie *My Big Fat Greek Wedding* came out, I had never laughed so hard. This was my family, only ours was the Italian version. My two best friends were my cousins Sal and Joe. Often, we'd have slumber parties; at four years old, I insisted that we say a rosary before we went to bed. As you can imagine, my cousins were not too happy with me and often convinced me to say only one decade. Afterward, I'd try to say the rest but fell asleep most of the time.

My mother assured me this was okay because my guardian angel finished it for me.

Life as I knew it was going to change dramatically when I entered the first grade. Kindergarten was not mandatory, and my mother thought I'd learn more at home with my grandmother. I learned to read and write, but my mother was called in to speak to the first-grade teacher about my "delay." Apparently, I had no clue who Cinderella, Sleeping Beauty, or the other fairy-tale characters were. I explained to my teacher that I knew all about Adam and Eve, Noah, and the Apostles; and I shared how I loved John, the beloved disciple, because he took care of Jesus' mother after His death. However, this did not impress my teacher.

As part of a big extended family, I was the center of attention. I think my aunts and uncles showered me with their love and their gifts because they felt sorry for the poor girl whose father left her and divorced her mother. I was spoiled! One of my aunts couldn't have children, and I became like a daughter to her. Whenever I learned a new prayer, I was placed on a table, and everyone who came into the house had to hear what little Felicetta did. This helped to shape my ego and pride early on. There wasn't anything I didn't think I could do, and my family encouraged this line of thinking.

My life took a turn when a man came to visit our home. I was so startled to see a strange man walk in the door that I immediately dove under the kitchen table. The only way they could get me out was when my Aunt Betty said a bug had fallen off her bag and she thought she saw it crawl under the table.

One More Child

I quickly scampered out and came face to face with Nicola DeSalvatore. It appeared that a wedding was in the works. In Catholic families—especially Italian Catholic families—divorce was a disgrace, and no one ever talked about my biological father. All I knew was that my grandmother carried a gun on her person. She said it was for protection. Much later I learned it was for *my* protection! My family feared that my real father would return to take me away.

Nicola not only married my mother, but he also legally adopted me. I don't remember having to learn to spell my new last name. He was a good cook, and other than the mishap in the kitchen when the Babluci (that's Italian for snails) escaped the pot and were crawling up the wall, I enjoyed almost everything he cooked. My grandmother and mother had spoiled me. If I didn't like a specific meal, my grandmother would get up and cook something else for me. This stopped when my new father came into the picture.

Soon we moved to a nice new house in Long Island, next door to my Aunt Betty and Uncle Tony and down the street from my Aunt Lillie and Uncle Sal. They lived in what I thought was a mansion, with a basement, three stories, and a vast garden. Uncle Sal would measure me yearly with his tomato plants to be sure I was growing. He also had an abundance of fruit trees, and the cherry were my favorite. We ate many meals in their garden patio outdoors under the lush trees, and I looked up to my older cousins Agatha and Josephine.

My grandmother still lived with us, as well as my mother's older brother Sal, who also worked in the city. My mother, father, and uncle left early in the morning to take the long train ride into work. I was still watched very closely, and friends outside of the family were discouraged. My grandmother continued to carry her gun. With my parents' combined cooking abilities, they decided to open a bakery. That meant my brothers and I could sometimes go to work with them on weekends, and we enjoyed this very much.

I loved the bakery. The smell and taste of freshly baked bread is one of my favorites, and to this day I enjoy baking—especially sweets. Soon I had two little brothers, seven and eight years younger. My brothers and I spent hours playing with bakery boxes, eating broken cookies that didn't make the display cases, and watching with awe as the flour mixers churned out new recipes. My father liked to experiment. My mother was a people person who charmed the customers with her kindness and her genuine interest in their lives. Soon they had regulars, and the business flourished.

My idyllic life was about to change, however. One day during third grade, I arrived home from school to see several cars in the driveway and heard yelling between my uncles and my father. The family thought my grandmother was overworked having to look after me and my little brothers while my parents ran a bakery full time, so we were moving—not down the street or to a nearby town but to another country: Canada! I was heartbroken to be separated from my grandmother and uncle and sobbed along with my mother for what seemed like hours. This was my first life tragedy.

I've since learned that the tragedies we face in

life make us strong, but I couldn't imagine then how I could get along without my grandmother. She was my rock. She was always there for me. Since my mother worked, it was my grandmother who greeted me when I returned from school, taught me my prayers, and emphasized a love of God and family. Moving away from her was almost like being separated from my mother.

We were riding down the interstate in our station wagon pulling a rather large trailer with all of our worldly possessions. I was sobbing as I looked out the open window, and I could hear my mother crying in the front seat. She hadn't wanted to leave either. In fact, none of us wanted to leave. I didn't understand adults.

My foundation was shaken. I couldn't believe God was allowing this to happen. I blamed God because I had learned that all things, came from God. In my mind, if we praised Him in all things, shouldn't we equally blame Him? At this point I didn't understand that only *good* comes from God, so I decided to test Him.

Through my tears, I began reciting Bible verses. One that came to mind was Matthew 17:20: *And He said to them, "Because of the littleness of your faith; for truly I say to you, if you have faith the size of a mustard seed, you will say to this mountain, 'Move from here to there,' and it will move; and nothing will be impossible to you."* So as we passed through the mountain terrain on our way to Canada, I began ordering the mountains to move in the name of Jesus. I watched.

Was He really there? Did He hear my cries?

Why didn't He move the mountain as He said He would? The mountains didn't move. I was disappointed and surprised. Ultimately, this placed a seed of doubt in my mind. A third grader doesn't have much theological understanding; kids take things literally. I didn't realize that I, with the conditional faith of a child, was in no position to test God. All I knew was that He had let me down in more ways than one!

After our move, my friends became my books, and I buried myself in reading. I've loved reading ever since my oldest cousin, Agatha, spoiled me with a gift. She was a college professor and taught French, and I was in awe of her. When I was eleven, she asked if I liked to read, and I said no. She was appalled and credited this to being assigned the wrong books to read in school. I have no idea whether this was true, but she took matters into her own hands when she took me shopping and purchased twelve books. The sheer volume overwhelmed me! What was I going to do with these books? The titles were many of her childhood favorites: *Rebecca of Sunnybrook Farm*, *The Little Prince*, the Trixie Belden series, *Treasure Island*, *Little Women*, and so many more. I soon fell in love with reading.

Ontario was an adventure, and it was there that I attended Catholic schools from grades four to six. We often had snow days, and my fondest memories were my father making an ice rink in our backyard for my brothers and me. Our family, now very small, became very close. There was no extended family meddling—no aunts, no uncles, and no cousins. Eventually, my parents reconciled with the rest of the family, and my grandmother and uncle came for short visits.

One life-changing event happened when I was invited to a friend's ninth birthday party. My parents finally approved although parties had been off limits until this point. I had lost the invitation and didn't have the address, so my friend said she'd meet me at the overpass. My dad dropped me off with strict rules to come back at a specific time. He saw my friend, and we waved happily as we walked toward her house.

When I arrived, I told my friend's mom that I had to leave at a certain time, and she said it would begin to get dark, so she would walk me herself. The party was so much fun that we all lost track of the time. When I finally noticed, I knew it was over an hour later than I had promised my father. My friend's mother walked me to the overpass, and I waited for what seemed like an eternity until I saw my dad's yellow station wagon whipping around the corner. He was furious with me and promised all types of dire consequences. When we arrived home, the house was shrouded in darkness, and I found my mother and brothers praying with lit candles for my safety.

The reunion was a sobbing mess. My family thought someone had taken me and worse. My parents made it clear that parties and friends in general were off limits, and they used this situation as leverage for decisions about my social life for many years. I revisited the incident many times and pondered different strategies I should have employed. Why didn't I ask my friend to write down her address and give it to my father? Why didn't I ask my friend's mother to call my parents with the address when I arrived? I don't know.

I believe some of the traumatic things that happen in our lives shape us. I knew I had ruined my chances of parties, and I used this life lesson to analyze situations and try to see good out of bad. I still had two best friends. I was a good student and made friends easily—even if we could be friends only at school. Soon, even this situation turned out to be temporary.

We discovered that my little brothers had allergies that were attributed to the weather and some of the foliage. The options were medication or moving to a warmer climate, and my parents opted for the latter. Our neighbors vacationed in Winter Haven, Florida. My mother said that any place with the word *heaven* in the name sounded like a good place. So three years after we moved to Canada we packed up and moved across the continent to Florida! A new adventure was soon to begin.

 ## Chapter 2
Life Circumstances

You formed my inmost being; you knit me in my mother's womb. I praise you, because I am wonderfully made; wonderful are your works! My very self you know.
—Psalm 139:13–14

Month Two

The baby is a little under an inch long and since conception has had unique DNA. The organs are present, the brain and spine continue to develop, and the heart is beating and pumping blood. Arms and legs, fingers and toes, and eyes and ears begin to form. He is unique—totally wonderfully made.

****

Leaving my two best friends was not nearly as devastating as leaving my grandmother had been. I knew everything would turn out well since our immediate family was intact. My parents wanted to buy a business and decided to drive around the small town looking at for-sale signs. They ended up purchasing a fried-chicken restaurant and a house nearby in a nice subdivision. They were excellent cooks and soon added Italian cuisine, so the restaurant was an almost instant success.

Since my parents were excellent at sewing, my wardrobe was one-of-a-kind and fit well. Humorously, I'd argue with my mother about dress length. When I would stand for a fitting, she'd pretend to make the hem much shorter. I believe this was her attempt at reverse psychology. While girls' hemlines were beginning to creep upward in the early 1970s, she may have realized it was better to appeal to my conservative nature by teasing me.

For some reason, my parents asked me if I wanted to attend a Catholic or public school, and I chose public. Why? Because the holidays would match my neighbors'. This set a crazy precedent for my parents deferring to me on many occasions by asking my opinion about weighty topics.

While I was a good student, somehow the differences in punctuation and grammar between Canada and the U.S. had me stumped. A summer school class before eighth grade helped me catch up, yet to this day I attribute my difficulty over punctuation to my schooling in another country, and I'm sticking to that story!

I tried hard. I was self-sufficient, full of self-confidence, and an avid reader. However, I would soon leave my fiction world behind and face the reality of middle school. It was during this time that my confidence in my looks would be shaken—an issue that would follow me well into adult life.

Normally, I didn't care what people thought—especially after my party fiasco. I learned to accept my family's values and set aside my true feelings. Yet somehow after moving to Florida, I found myself the center of attention and was happy to find my peers unbelievably friendly. It was here that I was thrust into the world of going steady. My parents made it very clear that boys were out. Until I was ready to get married, there was no discussion. Family values were lived each day, and there was no need for lectures or long-winded explanations. It was a time of simple black and white. My mom and dad said it, and we believed it. My parents didn't yell often, but when my father did, I felt the ceiling would fall in. I had a once-in-a-lifetime experience of this and did not want to repeat it ever again.

I babysat my little brothers because it was expected. I never felt imposed upon because I knew I held a responsible position in my family as the older sister. I began to notice that my school friends had a different set of rules than the ones I lived with. I wasn't ready to challenge the status quo, but my eyes were indeed opened. I started to see the differences between myself, being born into a "foreign" family, and my totally American or Americanized friends. No one else talked about their ethnicity. I was Italian, yet I knew nothing of my friends' heritages, and this seemed strange. I began to be influenced by friends who showed me that my parents' ideas were very old-school, especially compared to the freedom my friends enjoyed. They were allowed to visit each other's homes after school, attend slumber parties, date, and of course go to the Saturday night football games, all without repercussions or tears.

Only years later would I realize how right my parents were overall, in their protectiveness. While they had my best interests in mind, it was hard to see that at the time. Isn't it amazing how the older we get, the more we turn into our parents? Many things that we argued against in our youth often become foundational in our own parenting. As a mother, I too have deemphasized dating and urged my children to seek God first. His will for their lives can be discerned somewhat more easily without worldly distractions. How else can people move into the next steps of life if they don't spend time with God, getting to know Him and His ways?

The line in the sand imposed by my parents involved friends and dating. I began to argue about going to the home of my friend who lived across from our bus stop. My parents decided to take away the argument by picking me up at school, and I spent afternoons at the restaurant. If I asked about spending the night with a friend, the answer was always a resounding "No!" I soon learned that this was a losing battle, so I stopped asking. They were strict and micromanaged my life, which is a trait I have struggled against with my own children. I now realize that broken hearts and worse can happen when sensitive kids are the object of attention, especially in a school atmosphere where gossip abounds. Now I understand that parental protection takes courage, time, perseverance, and patience.

I understood that my parents were both my biggest champions and my biggest stumbling blocks in the world of boy meets girl. My father would throw out gems like "It's not that I don't trust you to walk out that door; it's that I don't trust anyone walking in." Another favorite was "It is better for you to cry now than for me to cry later."

I was ill prepared to face the world of middle school. The antics of the kids were foreign to me; I had lived a protected, sheltered life in Canada. In Florida people talked about dating and going steady, and I was astounded that their parents were on board. Soon I learned that the entire school—except for me—knew which girl a popular boy was going to ask to go steady. There was gossip surrounding his decision since he was torn between two girls. I was shocked to learn I was one of the girls!

Both a cheerleader friend and I had caught the eye of a cute boy. I tried to explain to my new friends that not only was I *not* interested in this person I didn't even know, but there was also no way my parents would let me go steady. Being melodramatic, I explained I'd be killed on the spot if I even told my parents, and I was only half-kidding. My friends told me to keep quiet or I'd be labeled as weird, so I should just play along. As a teen, I was now learning that I'd better stand up for myself or I'd be molded into a person I would not like.

My prayer life was still there; being raised in a Catholic family had ensured that my faith was intact. I had forgiven God for taking me away from my grandmother and had grown and flourished in Canada, but this boy-girl fixation was incomprehensible to me. While I was uncertain how to handle it, I didn't feel I could discuss it with my parents, which made me very uncomfortable.

Normally, I was the leader, self-confident and very capable. Thrust into a world I knew nothing about, I suffered needlessly—worrying I would be chosen and at the same time worrying I wouldn't be chosen. The gossip was that this young man was torn between my friend who was very pretty and the girl with the great personality, me—and he chose her. From that point forward, I believed I was not very pretty but I was fun! It's amazing how silly events can mold us for life.

I was embarrassed and hurting on the inside. No one likes public humiliation even if they are not the cause of the situation. Worst of all, I couldn't talk to my parents because I knew what they would say: "Why didn't you tell us? How could you let yourself get into this situation in the first place?"

I resolved to take matters into my own hands in the future. I should have told the boy I was not interested. I was *never* going to be put in such an awkward position again! I participated in class discussions, and I would tell people my opinions without much encouragement. I made it known that if I was ever interested in a guy, I'd let the guy know, and until that point, I was not interested. Setting these guidelines helped to shield me somewhat, and no one asked me out until my senior year of high school.

I was comfortable around boys since I grew up with male cousins close to my age, and I wasn't a flirt. Guys often chose me as a partner for class projects since I was an overachiever who would do most of the work. Eventually, I made some very good friends, both male and female. Life became happy again.

One day I was very upset about something I learned at school, and I accused my mother of lying to me about the Bible being truthful. Our science teacher said that we evolved through a process of evolution from molecules to man and that the world began with a Big Bang! I was shocked and so upset. I couldn't believe all the kids were sitting there and no one said a word. The fact that I wasn't saying anything either didn't occur to me—probably because I didn't know what to say.

My mother quickly took out the Bible, pointing me to the familiar chapters and verses of Genesis that spoke of a beautiful creation made by a creator God who loved us so much that He made this world for us and said that it was good. I was delighted to rediscover those verses and to remember that my creator God was personally involved in my creation. It was another pivotal point, a renewal of my faith.

My mother wisely counseled me to listen to the teacher, take the test, and give her the answers she wanted but to remember that it was a lie and that God created the world in six days. It is amazing that years later I would write curriculum that taught this very thing. In addition, my daughter and I would write a series of novels that taught the differences between evolution and creation in adventure stories so that children could understand that when God said He created something out of nothing, He was telling the truth.

To add to the joy of finally fitting in and finding a routine at school, I was delighted to learn that my grandmother was moving to Florida to live down the street with my uncle. She lived only two more years, but we were very happy to be reunited. She had aged considerably in the few years since I had seen her on a regular basis. I was back to riding the bus after school, and I would walk down the street to visit with her until I needed to go home and do homework. She still reminded me to pray and trust in God for all things. I don't remember having a great prayer life. I would pray but more to ask for things than to listen to anything God might be trying to teach me. In addition, leaving a Catholic school for public school didn't help.

My family didn't attend Mass, partly because of restaurant life and partly because my parents couldn't receive the sacraments since they were divorced and remarried. Certain things were never discussed, and divorce was one of those things. I never thought to ask my mother to take me to church.

My mother loved the Lord. She read her Bible and spoke to me about faith all the time, and she asked me questions that left me feeling uncomfortable, such as "Wouldn't you love to see Jesus?" My response was something like, "No. I'd freak out, Mom!" She would lament that she couldn't go to communion, and usually she would wish that she had never married my biological father. In my early teens, I was hit with a realization: "Mom, if you hadn't married my father, I wouldn't have been born!" After that, she stopped complaining. Many years later my parents would be reconciled with the church and have their marriage blessed. In fact, around the same time, they started attending a Catholic charismatic prayer group and did so for years.

Prayer was a way of life. I believed in God and was happy for my early upbringing. Yet the idea of feminism slowly crept into my life. It was the mid-1970s, after all. I didn't buy into the us-against-them mentality of radical feminism—just the competitive idea that I could do anything that a boy could. I was also pleased I had avoided all the teen drama by not dating, which allowed me to focus on the things that interested me. Books were still a big part of my life.

Other than my parents being ridiculously protective—no boyfriends, no dating, no attending school sports events, and no parties, especially no slumber parties—I was happy . . . until my father accepted my prom date invitation my senior year.

I had been asked to prom by a nice guy who was tall, a bit awkward with glasses too big for his face, and a year younger. Since I didn't have permission to attend any party, how would I tell my parents—but how could I turn him down? I felt bad for him, so I told him I wasn't permitted to date, but I would ask. Thankfully, in those days there was not the big fanfare that accompanies prom invitations today.

Later that day my dad returned from the bank and said, "The bank president said you were going to the prom with his son." I was shocked when he added, "If you want to go, that is okay with me." That was it—and I didn't even have to ask! It turned out that one of my good friends, Susan, was asked to prom by her family's exchange student, so we'd go together. I soon learned another boy whom I did like had planned to ask me to prom, but it was too late, and there was no way I could hurt my date. Here was the drama I had avoided for all those years.

By the end of my senior year, the boy who didn't take me to prom wanted to be my boyfriend if my parents allowed us to date. He was a year younger, and his family lived in the big house on the hill. He also went to the big Protestant church, where his father was an elder. Even though I had not been to church other than my two brothers' First Communions and Confirmations, I still considered myself Catholic, so that was a major strike against him. Yet he was fun, and for the first time a young man had captured my attention.

Our dating was limited to a specific day and time. Each Saturday after I worked at the restaurant, we could go out between 8:00 and 10:00 p.m. My parents monitored everything closely, and they were both unhappy because (1) he was not Catholic and (2) he was not Catholic. If there had been third and fourth reasons, they would have been the same.

My father believed that I needed to find a man to

marry, but this person was not acceptable, so he took matters into his own hands. He began introducing me to salespeople who frequented the restaurant, including suppliers who sold him food, paper goods, and more. One self-assured young man was a scuba diver and avid fisherman. He and my dad had much in common when they discussed good fishing spots because we had boats of various sizes and my dad loved to go fishing as time permitted. When I caught on to his not-so-subtle matchmaking attempts, I pleaded with my mom to make him stop!

When I think about this now, it is humorous, but at the time it was horrifying to think that my father was meddling in my future. Thankfully, God opened doors for me. and I was accepted to several colleges. My father believed college was a waste of time, and he vetoed the ones that were far away but agreed that I could go to Florida Southern in a nearby town. Somehow, they allowed me to live on campus. In addition to two very protective parents, I now had a very protective boyfriend who called often to check on me during my freshman year of college.

This turned out to be God's perfect plan for my life. My college years were a time of personal growth free of much of the dating drama. Without the boyfriend at home, along with returning home on the weekends to work at the restaurant, my father might not have allowed me to attend college, so I am grateful.

 ## Chapter 3
Intellectual Formation

But as it is, God placed the parts, each one of them, in the body as he intended.
—I Corinthians 12:18

Month Three

Your baby is about two to four inches long. The eyes, ears, mouth, and nose move into place, forming the face as the bones and muscles begin to develop. The brain grows, and brain waves can be recorded. The brain enables involuntary muscle movement, yet you won't feel it. The organs are forming, and he has fingernails developing and can even suck his thumb!

****

Before college began in the fall, we traveled to Italy to visit my father's childhood home on the Strait of Messina. It was beautiful! I loved the rocky terrain and the gorgeous blue-green water. We stayed with my Zia Maria and Zio Giuseppe, and I met my older cousins Rosario (Saro for short) and Giuseppe—who was married to an Iranian, Amal, who was expecting a baby. She loved my mother, who was quickly engaged in helping her through her pregnancy and ultimately attended the birth. The food was phenomenal. With a meat strike in progress, I learned to eat fish, which is now a favorite.

While on a walk down to the pier with my cousin to purchase the fresh fish, we saw a United States military ship. My cousin quipped, "Yankee go home!" I was shocked! Did he not realize the United States was an Italian ally? I quickly told him in no uncertain terms how wrong he was. He responded with his take on politics, and I had my first experience in debate on political views. He was surprised at my vehemence and said I shouldn't worry about such weighty topics. I was infuriated by the insult to my country and to me as a woman. Eventually, we agreed to disagree.

When I returned to the United States, I surprised my friends because my waist-length hair was now shoulder length. I'd had it cut and styled in Sicily and had also obtained a new wardrobe. The clothing and shoes were ahead of the styles at home, at least in my small slice of central Florida, and the changes were an outward signal that I was ready for a new chapter in my life.

I had it all planned. I'd marry my high school boyfriend

someday, but later—after I conquered the world. I loved to be helpful and to make a difference, and I needed a cause to make my life meaningful. I declared psychology as a major, but I couldn't stomach all those gross science labs. I knew I wanted to help people, and I was successful in counselling my friends—mostly through commonsense suggestions. Friends told me I should be an attorney because I could see both sides of an argument and get to the crux of the problem and to the solution quickly.

Instead, I became a teacher. I could counsel students and fellow teachers and be surrounded by books. What could be better? My first love, other than God, would be within the pages of a book. If it included mystery, adventure, and just a smidge of romance, all the better. But I wanted to keep romance to a minimum so I wouldn't be distracted from the challenge of solving the mystery!

I was planning to be a school principal one day. It would be the best of both worlds. I could be within the walls of academia and still have a hand in helping the world become a better place through working with kids. Truthfully, I don't know when the lines began to smudge in my aspirations, but I think it had something to do with a gorgeous, blond-haired, blue-eyed boy. And it wasn't the same boy I had been dating.

Going to a different college than your boyfriend is highly recommended if you want to focus on school. I joined a sorority the second half of my freshman year and met some incredible women whom I still consider my sisters. I graduated with a degree and multiple certifications, collected some prestigious awards, and enjoyed college life fully.

When I became the junior advisor, I received a monetary scholarship but also had to leave my sorority house to live with incoming freshmen and mentor them. God had a plan. I resided on the third floor, and I had to pass another advisor on the second, with her door regularly wide open and Christian music playing. She invited me to a Bible study, and I don't remember if I ever attended, but I did purchase and read a Bible. She and another friend asked me to pray a salvation prayer.

Because I was Catholic, they worried about my salvation. When I read the prayer, I felt that I had already committed my life to Christ first through my parents in Baptism, second in Holy Communion, and then in Confirmation—reaffirming my faith in Christ and His Church as a young person of my own free will. However, it was so long ago and because I agreed with everything in the wording of the prayer—to turn away from sin, to sin no more, and to profess Jesus as my Lord and Savior—I willingly prayed the prayer.

When I went home that weekend, I told my mother about the prayer and the Bible. She quickly glanced through it and said, "It's a Protestant Bible!" I didn't know there was a difference between Bibles. She soon informed me, "If you are okay with reading a Bible that is missing a few books, I guess I'm okay with it, but you should take one of our Catholic Bibles with all the books!"

Faith was instilled by my family, but I can't

truthfully say I had personal relationship with the Lord at this point in my life—not like I did as a child. I prayed but didn't ask for help for my day-to-day needs. Praying the salvation prayer made me think I had somehow slowly left God on the sidelines.

My junior advisor friend asked me about my boyfriend—specifically if I had prayed to the Lord about him. I had no answer for her. Pray for a boyfriend? That was an odd thing to say. She handed me a handwritten "True Love" prayer. Since I had a boyfriend, I gave the prayer only a cursory glance because I thought, "Oh, this is for people who don't have someone in their life—and I do." I placed the prayer in my Bible and promptly forgot about it for several years. This girl was such a wonderful example of Christian love. She had a generous heart and was kind and loving to everyone.

As president of my sorority the second semester of my junior year and the first semester of my senior year, I was in my element. I tempered the party atmosphere like a dictator, imposing fines on offending sorority sisters who decided a trip to the beach was better than working at a car wash to raise funds for our philanthropic project. Some opted to pay rather than work. Of course, it was all done in fun, and we enjoyed each other's company. I don't remember much drama. I enjoyed college life, school was manageable, working toward my degree in education was enjoyable, and I even considered my internships fun. It was a very happy time in my life.

The boyfriend side of my life, however, was not so good. After three and a half years of dating with both of us now in college and in different states, my boyfriend issued an ultimatum. It was a deal breaker for me, even with an engagement ring as a promise. It took some time to get over the hurt, but I got over it.

I know it was my mother's prayers and God's protection that saved me from marrying someone who ultimately wasn't right for me, even if I thought he was "the one." Now I warn my kids and anyone who will listen that if they have problems from the outset of a relationship, it isn't likely to improve. One major problem was my refusal to pass through the doors of his church because I was Catholic, even though I didn't attend weekly Mass.

The news of my breakup quickly spread; my college was small. I knew I wasn't ready or interested in another relationship, and I spread that word as well, similar to my stance in junior high. During this time, I attended Mass on campus, even though Florida Southern was a Protestant-affiliated college. Thankfully, at the time they provided a Catholic Mass on Sunday evening for Catholic students, and I began to attend the services. This is where I became acquainted with a baseball player by the name of Jeff, who was friendly and complimentary. Yet for some reason, I felt awkward about the attention.

I barely spoke to him, and if I did it was curt and walked back to my dorm as quickly as I could manage to escape his attention without being outright rude. He was nice, but I wasn't interested in a boyfriend. However, I knew there was something special about him. I was puzzled by how happy he seemed; he smiled all the time! I thought, "What's up with that? No one can be that happy!"

When my thoughts strayed his way, I convinced myself that as an upperclassman he was graduating soon and we'd go our separate ways. There was no reason to become attached to someone who lived hours away from me in Florida whom I'd never see again. Besides, I had another year of college to go.

However, Jeff attended my graduation; he had come back to visit some friends. One of my friends' parents from out of town had a hotel pool party for her graduation celebration. Jeff was there, and I was attracted by his kindness to some of the little kids swimming. A guy who liked kids? Interesting. We began to talk.

Jeff's major was physical education, and he hoped to land a job as a teacher when the hiring freeze ended. He was working in Fort Myers at a job that paid well but that he didn't enjoy. As the party was winding down, we sat outdoors and talked for hours. I probably did most of the talking, and he was a good listener. But things didn't end too well—he is humble, and I was full of myself. I was arguing a point and didn't understand his concern about his unworthiness to shape the minds of young children. His comments irked me since I was full of self-importance and couldn't wait to rule the world, even if I was starting with one classroom at a time.

He asked questions such as "What if I don't know enough to teach the kids?" and "What if I mess up?" I thought his line of thinking was flawed and let him know, speaking in a rather unkind manner.

Late-night conversation about weighty topics is never a good idea.

I wanted to conquer the world. I felt I was specifically created for the job of teacher—to shape young minds, to help little ones see their amazing future, to empower kids to think and have self-confidence. The late 1970s were a time of experimental education—coloring without lines, open classrooms without walls, and new math, which I thought was stupid because I could see that most of it didn't work. I couldn't wait until I had an opportunity to bring some of my brand of common sense back to the schools.

I didn't catch Jeff's subtle hints and concerns that were from a truly humble person. I was too busy discounting his real concerns and stating my own. When he left the hotel steps where we were chatting, I realized it was probably for the last time and felt a loss I couldn't understand. Why would I care if I saw this guy again? I barely knew him. Little did I know I would see him again, and I believe there was divine intervention at work.

Chapter 4
Reality of Life

God created mankind in his image; in the image of God he created them; male and female he created them.
— Genesis 1:27

Month Four

Your baby is about five to six inches long. The organs work, and the systems of the body are forming and functioning. He moves around, and there is plenty of room to turn, grasp, flip around, and kick. His face and heart are fully formed, and the lungs are developing. You can learn the baby's sex at around four and a half months or be surprised in the delivery room! He can hear sound, and the eyebrows, scalp, and hair begin to appear.

****

After graduation, I took a job teaching at a summer camp. The woods were fun, and the job met my criteria of being outdoors with little sweating and creature comforts like hot showers and beds in a camp dorm. The food was even good. When I returned from camp, I learned that my father had, on my behalf, accepted a job offer at the local junior high where I had interviewed prior to leaving for camp. It was the same school I had attended upon arrival from Canada all those years ago.

My dad accepting my prom date—and now my first job! It was too much. He was never going to stop, and why should he? He felt it was his job as a good Italian father to manage my life. Well, at least I was a college graduate with a job waiting in the fall, even if I wanted to teach elementary school. It was time to be practical since teaching jobs were scarce. The colleges did a good job of training teachers, but the demand wasn't there at the time, which is why I diversified my major.

In my family, my graduation meant a lot. I was one of a handful of college graduates in my large extended family, and I wanted my parents to be proud. At some point in my life, though, I was expected to be a stay-at-home mom; oddly, this didn't bother me at all. I was prepared to stay home once I had children; however, I planned to teach until then and eventually go back to teaching when they entered school. But that was not in the foreseeable future.

Returning home after the freedom of college was challenging. The ideal is to live at home for at least a year, work, and save money to get a financial reserve to launch yourself into independent living. It's a great idea but was difficult for someone who lived in a small town with a meddling father.

One More Child

My father tried to set me up with various men time and again. Each time I declined to go out with these would-be suitors, my level of frustration with being micromanaged grew. I was lonely and wanted to date—just not anyone my Dad picked out! I tried to hide my feelings from my parents. I didn't want them to worry, but I also didn't want them to interfere.

I missed the college scene. Gone was the swirl of the fun social life with all my friends. In the little town of Winter Haven, my social life was nonexistent, and my teaching job was demanding. I had to create individual evaluation plans (IEPs) each day in each subject for each of my twenty-five students. I often worked well into the evening preparing for the next day. My days blurred—working, eating, sleeping, and rising to repeat it all the next day.

My dream of teaching and changing the world one kid at a time was not quite what I imagined. The red tape of special education was a nightmare. While I loved helping the kids, I longed for more. It was then that I renewed my faith in God and found the "True Love" prayer my friend had given me, still tucked safely in my Bible. I began to pray it in earnest. Here is the first paragraph of that prayer:

> "Everyone longs to give themselves to someone—to have a deep soul relationship with another. To be loved thoroughly and exclusively. But, God to a Christian says, 'No, not until you are satisfied and fulfilled and content with being loved by Me alone, with giving yourself totally and unreservedly to Me. I love you, my child, and until you discover that only in Me is your satisfaction to be found, you will not be capable of the perfect human relationship I have planned for you.'"

This prayer sustained me and provided amazing comfort. It was at this point that I decided that if I could never find a true love on this earth, it would not matter because I had the love of God in my life. This decision was freeing, and my entire outlook changed.

I no longer worried about dating or who I might or might not meet. I was living life fully and was happy in the moment. I began to realize that rarely does anything work out as planned. I now believe this is a myth perpetuated by all the books I've ever read about planning: make a goal, set steps to achieving that goal, focus on the end, and everything will go well. Right. Patience is lost on the young. I was so impatient for something to happen!

A few of my teacher friends and I loved to go as a group to dance. This was the disco era. Most places didn't open until 9:00 p.m., and the closest place was an hour away, round-trip. It was frustrating, but living at home meant I followed the rules. The rule of going out between the times of 8:00 and 10:00 p.m. that I followed in high school and college just didn't seem doable at age twenty-one, so my parents raised the time to midnight. Since I lived at home, I abided by their rules.

Unexpectedly, we would soon have extended family living nearby. My father had offered a partnership to my mother's youngest brother, who would leave his construction job in New York and come to Florida to learn the restaurant business. They would begin with their one restaurant and then open additional stores. In fact, my father was in the process of looking at another place across town.

I thought the idea was fraught with problems, but no one asked my opinion like they had when I was a child. The store was manageable without my relatives. My uncle would cook with my dad, and my aunt would work the front with my mom. However, I was delighted to learn that my cousin Denise would come too. She was a year younger and all the things I was not. She was fun, had permissive parents, and knew her way around a dance floor and with the guys. Together we received lots of attention. She attempted to teach me the art of flirting, but it ended up being so humorous to me, and I failed miserably. She flirted enough for us both.

She was appalled by my dismal social life. For some reason, I told her about the guy I couldn't get out of my mind since graduation. I showed her a yearbook picture of Jeff and recounted our late-night debate. She insisted I write and apologize to him for my rudeness, but he never answered my letter.

Unfortunately, Denise didn't stay around very long because she missed her life and friends in New York. Yet her time in Florida served a purpose, and that was to encourage me to contact Jeff. The restaurant partnership dissolved soon after she left.

Soon after Christmas I was sharing an apartment with a college friend who taught elementary school and understood the role and responsibilities of being a teacher. She liked to stop and smell the roses, and I just didn't understand her. I would find her sitting on the small porch of our apartment, watching birds in the trees. I'd marvel that anyone could sit still that long and just watch in rapt attention. Years later when I thought about Theresa, this memory was in the forefront—how she taught me, without words, to just stop and enjoy life. I still struggle with sitting still, but when I do take time to enjoy the nuances of life that I often miss, they are precious. One of my wise pastors, Father Toner, says,

"We see God in the nature He created. Just watch the birds, the sky, the clouds, and feel the wind blow."

However, staying busy was drilled into me almost from birth by my parents' example. I needed to be productive and useful. I needed to make a difference. I was working toward changing the world!

One day I was shocked to see Jeff playing tennis at *my* apartment complex. He had left the higher-paying job in Fort Myers to take a teaching job in Winter Haven. Secretly, I hoped a tiny bit of that decision had to do with me. He knew I lived in Winter Haven. I cringed when I thought of that embarrassing letter I sent that he never answered, but I wondered if this was the answer to my prayer. Had God been slowly preparing my heart? Was it divine intervention that the cute guy who lived far away ended up moving to the same apartment complex? When Jeff saw me, he immediately walked over and asked me out under the pretense of Christmas shopping for his family; in fact, he took out his wallet and showed me one gorgeous blond, green-eyed girl after another. This surprised me. What guy carries pictures of his sisters in his wallet? Shopping convinced me to go out with him, but truthfully, I didn't need a reason. I took him to a megamall in nearby Orlando, and we had a blast. We walked around and talked and laughed as if we'd been friends forever. Amazingly, both my parents loved him as soon as they met him. Here was the Catholic my mother had been praying for!

Chapter 5
Happily Ever After

He made from one the whole human race to dwell on the entire surface of the earth, and he fixed the ordered seasons and the boundaries of their regions.

— Acts 17:28

Month Five

Your baby weighs about ten ounces and is six inches or longer. He is progressing and growing, vocal cords are forming, and he can cry! Movements are more pronounced, and you will know when he is awake and asleep. The immune system is developing, and a special protection over the skin and soft protective hair that covers the baby are forming. Fingerprints and teeth buds begin to form.

****

Jeff had seemed like a laid-back guy, but he had some very firm beliefs. One was attending Church on a regular basis. Our first real date included Mass and then dinner. No boy had ever asked me to Church as part of our date. I was touched by the gesture and thankful. Jeff was kind, considerate, and light-hearted, and I began to enjoy his friendship.

While I felt that I had a deep abiding faith in God, I didn't understand much about what I considered church rules with no purpose. My late-1970s education had focused on wide-open borders, feminism, and making up my mind on what I considered important. I felt my parents were unduly strict and thought church rules should be regarded as loose suggestions. What I missed was that like any good father, God has rules in place to guide, instruct, and protect us from things that will harm us and cause unhappiness here and now but also in our eternal destiny. These rules are not meant to bind but offer us true freedom (doing what we ought) that leads to happiness.

Any good parent knows to hold a struggling toddler's hand tightly in a crowded parking lot or while crossing the street rather than give in to the child's inclination to run where he will, for his own safety. We don't allow self-determination that could turn deadly. It's the same with God. The rules are in place to keep us from harm and close to His loving heart.

Jeff understood the rules very well. He was a weekly communicant and never missed Mass unless he was ill. His good example was a breath of fresh air, and when he proposed—a scant two months after our first shopping trip—I said yes! We were married eight months after our first date. I married my Prince Charming from those fairy tales I never learned as a kid. I could scarcely believe I had a real prince.

As I write this, we have celebrated thirty-nine years of marriage, which have been a blessing. Have there been problems? Naturally! I'm one very determined woman of Italian descent, married to a man of German-Irish descent. It makes me laugh when people desire world peace. Let's just aim for peace within families first!

After we married, we moved to Fort Myers—about two and a half hours away from Winter Haven. While I was sad to leave my family, I knew this was a good move for Jeff and me. I needed a little space from my parents so I could learn to be a married woman. I accepted a job at a middle school in Fort Myers. It seems that God also had this in His plans for my life—I understood middle-school kids, and it turned out my dad's job selection for me the year before was a perfect one!

My parents had my younger brothers and a restaurant to keep them busy. Soon after Jeff and I moved, my parents purchased property in the neighboring town of Cape Coral and planned to build a house there when they retired a few years later. It gave Jeff and me time alone before my family moved nearby. Jeff's family lived within walking distance, and they often stopped in unannounced. We lived in a tiny house, had some savings, and were comfortable and very, very happy.

One of my life regrets is the brief time I took birth control pills. As a Catholic, I should have known better, yet I never heard anyone talk against birth control in church. My doctor prescribed birth control, and I gave little thought to the Church's teaching. I don't even remember talking to Jeff about it, even though it would affect him as well. We were not sexually active before marriage, which was one reason for the short engagement.

Years later I would learn about the detrimental effects of birth control on women and how often birth control fails when I was given an audio of Dr. Janet Smith's talk about the dangers of birth control, "Contraception: Why Not." I later learned of the research by Human Life International with statistics that over half of first-time abortion seekers were using birth control.[1]

When I was a young married woman, my mother gave me a copy of Pope Paul VI's *Humanae Vitae*[2] (Latin for "Human Life"), written in 1968. (I find it significant that I am publishing my book on the fiftieth anniversary of this document.) This small book spoke about the Church's constant position that contraception use is wrong because it prevents babies from coming into existence.

Few people know that until 1930, all Protestant denominations agreed with the Catholic Church's position that contraception is sinful. In 1930 at the Lambeth Conference, the Anglican Church announced that contraception would be allowed. Soon all the other Protestant denominations followed. Today, only the Catholic Church and a few smaller independent Protestant churches uphold the historic Christian position on contraception.

Humanae Vitae accurately predicted that the contraceptive mentality would result in an increase in infidelity, decrease

---

[1] Fr. Shenan J. Boquet, "Contraception Leads to More Abortions," Human Life International Website, October 30, 2017, https://www.hli.org/2017/10/contraception-leads-abortions/.

[2] Pope Paul VI, *Humanae Vitae*, 1968, http://w2.vatican.va/content/paul-vi/en/encyclicals/documents/hf_p-vi_enc_25071968_humanae-vitae.html.

in morality, and the loss of respect for women. The culture in the 1960s began the sexual revolution, and divorce rates rose in marriages where contraception was practiced. This certainly answers the sarcastic question some people ask, "What does an old, celibate man in Rome know about real life in America?" Obviously, the culture today shows that Pope Paul VI knew quite a bit!

Jeff and I talked about having children, yet we didn't discuss a timeline. I believed birth control was the norm for a married couple, and I didn't consider prayer or even agree with the *Humanae Vitae*, although it obviously planted a seed. Sadly, I was a cafeteria Catholic, picking and choosing the teachings that I liked.

In addition, our required premarital training was very weak, and I remember paying little attention to the couple expecting their eighth child as they discussed natural family planning. Obviously, we thought *that* didn't work! We didn't realize that the people teaching the class *chose* to have a large family. They were "open to life"—a term I was unfamiliar with at the time. Natural family planning is not birth control but is a method employed by a couple when there is a serious reason to space children. It is over 90 percent effective when used correctly.[3] My niece used this method while in medical school and later during part of her medical residency when she served in the Navy. She was opposed to birth control pills on moral grounds, as well as being concerned about the side effects. I'm extremely proud of Marie and her husband, Matt, for their example to other doctors.

Before Christmas in 1979, the year we were married, Jeff asked me to get off birth control. He wanted to start

---

[3] "The Effectiveness of NFP," Couple to Couple League Report, https://ccli.org/docs/effectiveness-student-guide-pages.pdf.

a family, and I agreed. The middle school where I taught was troubled, with rampant discipline problem. Kids often fought in the halls, and female teachers were instructed to call the male teachers and warned not to break up fights. I loved my students and found I could make a difference in their education, but I knew that when I became pregnant, I would stay home and not return to school to teach the next year.

On our first wedding anniversary, I was five months pregnant. Before our child's birth, I decided to go visit a priest in confession; it was another weight taken off of my shoulders. Now I felt that I was at peace with the Lord, I had renewed my covenant with Him, and He had provided for me—even as an uninformed sinner. Don't ever assume your children understand the reasons why you do the things you do—in all matters, but especially in faith. Often, we instruct our children when they are little and expect that instruction to last. Instead, we must encourage our children to continue to study, pray, and more importantly develop a lifelong relationship with our Lord.

Our son Neal was born on Christmas Eve. I was delighted to have this baby; for weeks I'd hold him even when he was sleeping. I kept walking by the mirror in our home just to see a baby in my arms. Two years later, our daughter Christina was born on the same blessed day. Two Christmas Eve babies—what are the odds? I felt they were very blessed to be born on the eve of the celebration of our Lord's birth!

Yet something wasn't right with my firstborn; Neal was missing some important milestones. Soon I would learn that the challenges I had faced up to this point were nothing compared to the road ahead.

Chapter 6
Devastating News

You know me inside and out, you know every bone in my body; you know exactly how I was made, bit by bit, how I was sculpted from nothing into something.

— Psalm 139:15

Month Six

Your baby is about ten inches long now, and you will feel his movements more often. He may have hiccups as the nervous system is nearly formed. The lungs develop, and he will practice breathing. He can feel and respond to pain and recognize your voice, as well as other familiar voices. His eyes open and close, and he even has eyebrows.

****

Something was wrong—very wrong—with my son. Charting his growth in a baby calendar keepsake book helped me realize he wasn't smiling, he wasn't crawling when he should, and he definitely was a "soft" baby with little muscle control to hold himself up.

When I mentioned my concerns to Neal's pediatrician, he wasn't alarmed. He said I was looking for things since as a teacher, I was familiar with developmental signs of growth. Looking for things? What mother looks for problems? Neal finally walked at thirteen months, well within normal parameters, but the main issue was his speech delay.

At four years old, Neal still wasn't talking clearly. He was talking, but we couldn't understand what he said. My two-year-old daughter would translate as if they had their own secret language. However, she spoke in sentences, and we could understand her perfectly. I hounded the pediatrician at every visit, and finally he agreed we should have Neal tested.

When the test results came in, we had to drive to Tampa, about two hours from our home, to meet with the physician who had analyzed them because he wanted to examine Neal. Questions swirled in my mind, and I knew the results could not be good since we were going to another doctor.

The doctor examined our son and then showed us small signs on his feet, hands, small rolls, etc. that we had never noticed. We learned our son had Mosaicism. I was familiar with Down syndrome yet knew nothing about Mosaicism. How could it be? I felt my world begin to crumble.

People with Down syndrome have an additional

chromosome in their cells. In Mosaicism, most cells are normal, but some carry an extra chromosome. Neal had a very small percentage of cells carrying the extra chromosome. This news was devastating. I was in shock. I couldn't process it. Yet I remembered the verse Mark 8:34: *Whoever wishes to come after me must deny himself, take up his cross, and follow me.* I wasn't sure I could follow in those steps. The cross was way too heavy; and without turning to God, I found I was immobilized, unable to cope. Jeff took the news so much better than I did. He smiled and hugged our son and said, "Everything will be okay."

On the other hand, I began to ask the doctor a series of questions. Since this type of diagnosis was rare at the time, no one had definitive answers. There was no database, no Internet, no Google or Siri to answer our questions. One percent of Neal's cells carried an extra chromosome, but what did that mean? Would he be able to take care of himself? Could he drive? Would his speech ever be normal? Could he do basic calculations? The doctor had an apologetic look on his face and repeated, "I don't know."

This was not what I wanted to hear. I expected answers from the specialist. Thankfully, today there are online sources that can help parents understand what to expect. For us, every day was an adventure.

We returned to pick up our daughter at my parents' restaurant in Winter Haven, and I sobbed in my dad's arms as they kept asking me what was wrong. Jeff filled them in and said, "Everything is going to be okay; he's our special child."

My husband was a rock of support and love, yet

as I cradled my two-year-old daughter, I knew my life would never be the same. I literally mourned for an entire year. I could not believe God had given me a "special" child! I was very upset with God and didn't think of this as a gift or a blessing. My pastor, Father Toner, often shares a story of a mother with a severely handicapped child who needs care in everything from eating to dressing to basic necessities. When he visits her home, he is always astounded that she tells him her child is a blessing. I know the story was meant to make me feel better, but this added guilt since I didn't feel the same. I was not a heroic mother.

I couldn't see that God in His infinite wisdom and mercy had perfectly prepared me not only to parent but also to teach this child. My degree was in elementary education with a certification in specific learning disabilities as well as early childhood education. If I had taken a step back and looked at my credentials, I would have realized I was well qualified. Yet I was blinded. All I knew was that my dreams and aspirations for my son died that day.

The news took me into a deep depression that I didn't recognize at the time. All the happiness in my life drained away. I could only focus on what I didn't know. I started looking back at Neal's baby journal and chastising myself for not seeing the signs. Neal didn't sit up unassisted until he was over six months, and he didn't roll over until about eight months. He didn't smile or laugh until he was eight months old; I just thought he was a serious baby.

Neal had difficulty following directions and obeying us, and he was impulsive. I couldn't figure out if it was a lack of understanding or if he was a stubborn and willful child. It was hard to know because of his lack of communication skills. He said "No!" to everything. He took all my patience, and by the end of the day, I was exhausted. Jeff would come home and take the little ones outside to give me a much-welcomed break. Our neighbor often teased that she didn't know who had more fun playing—my children or my husband.

Soon after we received Neal's diagnosis, we had an unexpected visitor. One of our college friends and his wife came with their son, who was about two years old. This little boy was very precocious, and I watched with a teacher's eyes as he played and interacted with my two children. I watched his use of fine motor skills, and on a whim, I asked his mother if she thought her son was gifted.

She smiled and started sharing all the skills her little boy demonstrated, including using the magnetic ABCs on the refrigerator, sounding out the letters, and forming simple words. Yes, I assured her, he was way ahead developmentally. After they left, I had another mental struggle, asking, "Why didn't you give me the gifted child, Lord?" I would have loved to have a child I could challenge.

These parents had no idea what to do! It was a heartfelt prayer of desperation. In my downward spiral the Lord gave me, an ungrateful sinner, an answer: "I give special people special children."

Months later I told Jeff what I felt the Lord had revealed to me. He said he was already aware we had been specially chosen, but he had remained silent, knowing I'd realize it at some point. This realization that God had chosen us was a wake-up call, something the Lord continued to work out in me. I had my answer, and I knew the Lord would equip me and not let me down. He has remained faithful! Yet I was still overwhelmed.

I could cope with only one day at a time. I was a planner and liked to think about the future, but now the future looked very dim, especially for my precious little boy. I knew he'd have a hard time in school. I kept thinking if I could get him to eighteen and skip school, that would be the answer, but I had no idea how to avoid school. Homeschooling was not something I considered at the time. Worry for his future loomed in the forefront of my thoughts. Would he eventually be able to live on his own? Would he be able to drive? Like a looped video, these thoughts plagued me. I was unable to answer these questions for myself, and it seemed no one else could answer them either.

Basically, I was grieving. In my downward spiral, I needed someone to blame. I blamed my pediatrician for requiring us to go to Tampa to get the diagnosis from a stranger without preparing us for the tragic news in some way, so I promptly changed doctors. I hadn't been prepared for that appointment, so I was blindsided. I didn't have a good set of questions to ask the expert. Maybe the pediatrician thought the geneticist would have the answers, but he did not. I will never know. I have long ago forgiven the doctor—he did what he felt was best at the time, I am sure.

One More Child

I am forever thankful for a decision we made on the spot at the geneticist's office not to have additional blood work performed on Jeff and me to see whose genetic "fault" caused "the Mosaicism". The doctor recommended the test to give us an informed conscience for our decision on having more children. We decided we didn't need to know, and I think in my heart I knew I was no longer open to having any more children. During this time of profound sadness, I also knew I should not make any rash decisions.

Another doctor who advised us was my OB-GYN, who recommended that Jeff and I take permanent precautions to avoid more children, via a vasectomy. I knew in my heart that what he was saying went against Church teachings, but I still went home and shared the news with my husband. He wasn't excited about the thought and said we needed to get spiritual counsel. We didn't have a relationship with the pastor of our church at this time. He had been Jeff's pastor growing up, yet neither of us felt comfortable talking to him. In hindsight, if we had, he would not have approved of our decision.

As it happened, our church was having a mission, and an out-of-town priest was coming to teach. This was perfect! We wouldn't need to talk our parish pastor, and I thought a mission priest would somehow be more holy since he spent the bulk of his time evangelizing and teaching people to get closer to God through his mission work.

The meeting with the mission priest was a disaster. The mission was wonderful, and his words were inspiring. However, when I entered the pastor's office for a private meeting with him (after waiting for four hours with two children under the age of four), he didn't seem to be a patient man. My son, who had been good while we had waited, was horrible in the office. He ran around impulsively, tried to turn the lights off and on, and pretty much gave the poor pastor a picture of a slice of my life with a cooped-up four-year-old.

He asked me, "Is he always like this?" I quickly explained Neal's diagnosis and that he had trouble listening and I wondered how much he actually understood. He nodded as I spoke, seeming deep in thought. Finally, he said, "God wouldn't want you to have more than you can handle." He agreed we needed to take precautions because we couldn't possibly want another child with genetic problems. So much was wrong with his statement, but I didn't stop to analyze or think about his words. All I heard was "Yes— you should go through with your plans." For some reason, my heart was heavy when I left the office; but it would be many, many years before I could digest what had taken place.

When my husband returned from work, I recounted the mission pastor's words. That was exactly what Jeff needed to hear. As cradle Catholics, for us the priest is an authority. If he said it was okay, then it had to be okay. This demonstrated that we didn't know our faith. Even years later I don't blame the priest for our bad decision. He advised us badly, but it was our free will. God gave us free will to decide whether to have more children or not have any more children. I blame myself. I take full responsibility for the action.

One More Child

Did we ask anyone else? Did we really get on our knees and pray? No. We walked into this situation on our own accord. We knew better. How could we not?

We had no idea if we could have any more children, let alone if the child would have Mosaicism. In fact, if we wanted to avoid pregnancy, we could use natural family planning. Instead, we chose vasectomy. This priest had given us a green light on the need to avoid pregnancy. So why did we feel guilty?

We didn't tell anyone because we are private people. However, in the back of our minds was the knowledge that the decision we made was against church teachings. It was as if this sin had to be hidden, similar to Adam and Eve hiding from God in the Garden. The only person who knew about our decision was my sister-in-law, whose husband had done the same thing. While she had wanted another child, he did not. His own family was large and had many traumas that he felt were made worse because of the number of children in the family. So they had made a deal, prior to their second child's birth. Since they had a boy already, if the baby was a girl, they would stop there. My sister-in-law lost the bet, and she could not talk him out of it. At the same time, she had all she could handle at the moment with a two-year-old and a newborn. I was upset for her, especially if she wanted more children, but at this point I was worn out. I reasoned that she had a boy and a girl, just like me, and our children were very close in age. We had all we needed. I had no regrets or feelings of remorse, but the stifling guilt and remorse did eventually come years later.

Chapter 7
Coming Home

Before I formed you in the womb I knew you.

— Proverbs 20:12

Month Seven

Your baby's weight is between two and four pounds, and he's starting to develop fat. Movement will decrease as he begins to run out of room. He can see, hear, and taste; and the brain is continuing to develop rapidly, along with the nervous system.

****

My focus was on Neal. I was on overdrive. I had a purpose and mission, and my obsession was helping my son. I had Neal tested through the public school system; despite my experience as a teacher, I felt the need to give it a try. However, as I feared, his IQ tests were at such a vast range that the scores were invalid. When I questioned a particularly low score, I was told they had administered a test for the hearing-impaired using sign language. Seriously? Neal could hear just fine, and he didn't know sign.

With the doctor's recommendations and diagnosis, we began two days a week of speech therapy and one day of occupational therapy at the hospital. While there I met Toni, who, like me, needed a friend. I soon learned that her only child was deaf. Her daughter was in speech therapy because Toni and her husband wanted her to fit into a hearing world; they had researched and found that speech therapy was a good start. Toni understood me and all I was going through, and we became good friends.

God provided once again, although I had not prayed specifically for this need. He knows our every desire, both spoken and unspoken. He knew I'd spiral down into a deeper depression without someone outside of my family to talk to. While Toni and I had different ideas of how to approach our needs, she became my rock. They ultimately decided to send their daughter to a boarding school that specialized in teaching deaf children to deal with a hearing world. I opted for an entirely different solution. Yet we supported each other in our decisions.

I found an elite preschool that did more than

organized play. With a background in preschool education, I knew what to look for. This school checked off all the boxes, even down to the building nestled into a wooded yard with a wonderful and inviting courtyard. I promptly enrolled Neal and soon my daughter, Christina, as well.

During this time, I had Neal tested extensively. After several meetings with the public school personnel, I eventually decided that they had misdiagnosed Neal. They stated his IQ was so low he had to attend a class with the hearing impaired, the speech delayed and those who were also mentally challenged. After my experiences as a teacher, I should not have been surprised. Neal could hear and could communicate in his own way, and speech therapy helped somewhat. He had a long way to go to articulate his words, but he spoke and knew what he was saying. We were the ones who must be trained to understand. I knew that Neal did not need sign language. Their recommendation was flawed, especially since the range of scores varied widely. At this point I was at a loss for words, an oddity for me, and I determined to petition the special needs department head at the school board.

I felt like I was back in my teaching days with the administration labeling kids with inaccurate classifications. This doesn't always happen—far from it—but if a parent or teacher wants to disagree, my experience was not favorable. This time I was fighting for my son. The department head told me the crux of the issue: "You cannot make a unilateral decision on your son's placement." My response? "I know what the word unilateral means—and without my permission, you cannot place my child in a classroom for the mentally impaired just because you want the state dollars that come with this classification." I asked if I was right, and he said yes. Instead of pursing another round of testing, I enrolled Neal in a private Christian school—the only one in town with an open door for struggling learners. The principal, whose wife was the kindergarten teacher, assured me that I could help provide materials or help in the classroom. Soon Neal was settled in and was doing well. Christina still attended the private preschool, and now my days were my own.

I discovered an entire new world of shopping, days at the hair salon, and tennis; I even hired a tennis coach at the insistence of a friend. While all this was fun, I felt my purpose was taken from me since my kids needed me for only part of the day. When we considered building a house at the other end of town, I had many sleepless nights wondering about my kids' schooling and became concerned about finding another school that would meet Neal's needs.

Eventually, we hired a private psychologist to administer tests and found that Neal's IQ was normal, which I had surmised after working with him on a computer. Back in the early days of the PC revolution, I purchased a Commodore 64 computer so that my son could use some of the newest learning games. He was quick and loved it. I recall trying to remember how to print, which at the time required a series of function keys. F-something meant print. After Neal completed a game for which he would receive a cool certificate, I told him that I didn't remember how to print.

While I was searching for the computer manual, he reached over and hit the necessary keys, and the printer began to whirl. I was shocked! We had printed only one time before, and he remembered the command.

Neal made great progress in the hospital therapy sessions. The psychologist gave me the name of a lady whose husband was a doctor and who was homeschooling her daughter with nearly the same diagnosis as Neal. Chris was delightful, and she became a friend and mentor. At that point, the idea of homeschooling came onto my radar screen and I began thinking it was an option for us. Neal was to repeat kindergarten at the suggestion of his teacher. I knew that he thrived with one-on-one instruction, and now I needed to persuade my husband.

Since my degree was in special education, it made sense for me to teach him, but the idea did not appeal to me initially. In college, the one class I absolutely detested was speech therapy; I sold that textbook as soon as class ended, while keeping many of my other college books. I now wished I had listened and learned more. Amazingly, my sister-in-law Janice had decided to homeschool. In fact, she was worried about telling me because she thought that as a teacher, I would be negative toward her decision.

The only other time I heard about homeschooling was from friends who were not the best disciplinarians. When they asked me about homeschooling, I advised against it, thinking that if they couldn't even get their kids to go to bed, schooling them at home might not be the best idea. I now regret giving them that advice because we went on to enjoy over thirty years as a homeschool family.

Jeff suggested that we try homeschooling mid-year, and if it didn't work out we could place Neal back in school the next year. Neal flourished and didn't mind not going to school. In fact, he loved having me to himself. Christina was still at the preschool. Now, instead of lunches out and playing tennis, I was working with my five-year-old, and he was making progress. Some subjects were a struggle, and we used many manipulatives. He still attended speech therapy and occupational therapy.

Neal was high-functioning intellectually, so he would have slipped through the cracks in a public or private school. He needed the one-on-one attention that homeschooling provided. Other than some learning delays in academics rather than life skills, he was very near normal. Now we were a homeschool family, and our days were immersed in this lifestyle. I never looked back, and I planned to bring Christina home to begin kindergarten when the new school year began.

When we moved to our new house, we had a pool party. My children's friends were a mix of homeschool and preschool kids. It was an eclectic group, and I realized that I loved being friends with everyone. However, some felt intimidated by the idea of homeschooling. They thought I was saying I was a better parent. That was so far from the truth! However, both my friends and my extended family supported my decision to homeschool Neal but thought I should place Christina in school. I wanted

One More Child

us to be a family and learn together, and my husband agreed.

Soon I had many friends who homeschooled; the added bonus was that they were Christians! I was the only Catholic in a group of Protestants, mostly Baptists. I loved these women. They opened their homes, they were genuinely kind, and they all had three children at the most. Small families were the norm.

I was on a committee to help with the new school year by planning for field trips and other events such as unit-study co-ops held in each other's homes. As I was standing in the kitchen of a friend's beautiful home after the meeting, I looked around at the women I now called friends, and I was pleased at my decision and amazed at how the Lord had finally brought me peace. God provided beautiful families for my two children to interact with and learn alongside. Finally, I realized that with my education, the Lord had equipped me to teach both of my children. Nothing is wasted.

As we sipped coffee, one of my friends was sharing how very upset she was that she couldn't have any more children. The others were comforting her, and then one by one, they all shared the news they carried secretly. None of them could have more children. The common reason? Vasectomies! Every one of their husbands had succumbed to the culture's notion that they had enough children, and vasectomy was the next logical step. I was greatly disturbed deep within my spirit. I could have chimed in at any time, "Me too! Me too!" but I didn't. I was stunned, and I was not ready to share my secret.

My mind was racing as I processed this information. Every one of these lovely women who loved God . . . wait, all of us women who loved God had agreed with our husbands to take permanent action against having more children. Why? Why had we who professed to follow Christ in everything chosen to turn our backs on this one very important and foundational purpose of marriage, the procreation of children? How could we be open to God's will in our lives but not open to His will when it came to the number of children? I was quiet the rest of the evening; if anyone noticed, no one said anything.

We had all been dealt lies, and the roots were in feminism, provided through our worldly education. We were taught that women could do as well as or better than men. Women shouldn't stay at home and raise their children; it was an inconvenience, a burden, and a waste of education and talent. If women wanted children, they should have no more than one or two, and they should go back to work as soon as they could. I had planned to return to work, and if not for my son's academic struggles, I would be teaching. Entrenched in these thoughts was anxiety, fear of failure or being held back, and an underlying spirit of competing with men.

Years later, I would read John Paul II's Apostolic Letter *On the Dignity and Vocation of Women*. This wonderful document is a must-read for every woman. It traces the significance of strong women throughout the Scriptures, ties in the woman in Genesis to the woman in the New Testament, and explains how the "Yes" from Mary, through her own free will, brought our Savior and Lord Jesus Christ into the world. Womanhood is elevated to sanctity purified by God. *"Christ became a promotor of women's true dignity* and of the *vocation* corresponding to this dignity.*"*[4] In the Bible, we learn how at times this caused scandal.

This document states that God instituted marriage "as an indispensable condition for the transmission of life to new generations, the transmission of life to which marriage and conjugal love are by their nature ordered: 'Be fruitful and multiply and fill the earth and subdue it' (Gen. 1:28)."[5]

Using birth control of any type and having a vasectomy go totally against God's plan for marriage. Sterilization takes away the sanctity of married life and reduces it to its lowest form.

As my thoughts became increasingly rooted in Catholic theology, it became more difficult to stand firm in a group of women who tried to convert me to Protestantism. Explaining that I had accepted Christ multiple times was still not enough, and I listened politely as they brought up point after point about the errors of teaching within the Catholic Church. I then began to study my faith more deeply. What did

---

[4] "Pope John Paul II, "On the Dignity and Vocation of Women," 1988, section V, paragraph 12, http://w2.vatican.va/content/john-paul-ii/en/apost_letters/1988/documents/hf_jp-ii_apl_19880815_mulieris-dignitatem.html.

[5] "On the Dignity and Vocation of Women," section III, paragraph 6.

we believe about Mary? Did we worship statues? Did we pray to the dead?

The answers were easy to find. I explained that we believed that Mary was the Mother of Jesus, and therefore we could not, as humans, love her more than Jesus did. No, we didn't worship statues, only God. And no, we didn't pray to the dead. As a student, I loved learning, and this was no different. These women opened my heart to a thirst for God, and for that I am eternally grateful.

Our new home on two and a half acres was the perfect place to raise a family, and we were excited about our plans. The one thing this property didn't have was cable TV, so we had many years with antenna service on our television and only the basic channels. This was before the Internet, streaming television, and affordable satellite networks. The children and I turned to reading books, playing games, and watching carefully selected videos, many with godly content. I bought every book on the saints that I could find, and once again I was among my childhood friends and teaching my own children. It was a very happy time for all.

Within a few years, my parents were building a house in a neighboring town. Jeff was their builder, and we soon would enjoy extended family like my experiences growing up in New York. I was happy that my children would have two sets of grandparents to love and nurture them, and especially happy that Jeff's sister Janice made frequent trips to our coast and we to hers in Fort Lauderdale. Our children learned many of the same things, and we often combined our family trips with educational field trips. My two younger brothers and Jeff's additional three sisters, while not homeschooling families, all supported our decision to homeschool.

We loved our new church, which was closer to our home, and I began teaching religious education. I became familiar with the pastors and often had Father Toner to the house for dinner so that we could enjoy riveting theological conversations. I was studying the Scriptures and church teaching when I realized there was so much I didn't know. I felt a need to confess our decision to have a vasectomy yet was unsure about how to do so. How I could compartmentalize and rationalize poor decisions astounds me now.

At the time, I refused to dwell upon the past, especially since my relationship with God was growing positively. My depression had been replaced by a focus and a plan for my children. Why couldn't I just go on with my life? The secrecy and guilt I still harbored, along with a nagging feeling that the decision to have the vasectomy was wrong, persisted. To dispel this notion, I reminded myself that I had asked the permission of a priest and that made it okay. I never spoke about this to my husband. We were busy parents of little children. Who had time for deep introspection about faith? I didn't know our parish priest well enough to discuss this mistake.

Our conscience is a gift from God, and it can be developed or undeveloped. Without learning and growing in the love of God, studying His word, praying, going to church, and living life with a focus on heaven, life is empty. I wanted true communion with my God in every sense of the word. I craved to know Him deeply. He knew this hunger, and He had placed it in my heart as a child. My conscience was pricked, and I had a choice to make, so I prayed.

One Sunday, people from Marriage Encounter came to church and invited anyone interested to sign up for a retreat. Many women tried to make their husbands go, yet I was not among them. While we were at the parish for coffee and donuts, I sat with a group of friends, watching our children playing nearby. One pointed out my husband signing us up for the retreat! Jeff earned super-husband points in the eyes of my friends that day. I was not sure what he had in mind. We were told that Marriage Encounter events were for good marriages, not troubled ones. I agreed our marriage was good, and my husband confirmed that we were not going because he was upset, just because he thought we needed to deepen our commitment to each other. I went, but I was not happy.

At the weekend, certain events happened that I believe were God-ordained and that helped us connect as a couple. I learned that my husband was not a stickler for rules the way I was; in fact, when we were sent to our room to discuss certain topics, he crossed them out and wrote his own question at the top. At least I saw this as humorous, or our first night wouldn't have gone so well. Jeff did have some concerns, and a one-to-one retreat was the best way to get my full attention without the children.

He wasn't happy about my volunteering outside of the home. He felt some things were okay but others were getting out of hand. While my kids were in preschool, I had become involved in Junior League. It was fun, like a continuation of my sorority days. I met other women who volunteered within the community, and there were several fund-raisers during the year. I had recently joined the education committee, since I was a former teacher and now a homeschool mom.

I was soon supposed to fly to the state capital to meet with legislators and the Secretary of Education of Florida and present some of my concerns about public education. Jeff didn't like the idea of me flying to Tallahassee or all the other times I had left him with the children to volunteer in different town events. Jeff wanted me to quit Junior League and was ready for a fight. The little interaction I had had with local legislators as well as certain educational reform books I had read showed me it would take divine intervention for changes to take place. While I loved the kids and believed many teachers are heroic, I thought the educational bureaucracy was muddled in red tape. I readily agreed to quit. While the retreat was a blessing for our marriage, I felt that something was missing. That something was my deep concern about the vasectomy, but when I finally brought it up, Jeff reiterated what I had considered through the years: we had received a priest's blessing.

About a year later we were invited to a Cursillo weekend, a Christian apostolic mission similar to Marriage Encounter except that each person goes separately. There is a men's weekend and a women's weekend. First my husband went, and then I attended the next weekend. The idea for a married couple was to commit deeply to the Lord, their family, and themselves. The husband, as the spiritual head, was asked to attend first and not share the events that transpire on the retreat. The retreat was set up to give us time to focus in silence and prayer.

In deep prayer, I felt my eyes were opened. I had time to pray before the Blessed Sacrament, and I wept when I saw the picture of the Divine Mercy—a life-sized image of Jesus with red and white rays coming from His heart. Jesus is depicted as open to our suffering and offering us His resurrection as mercy for sinners. I knew the chaplet of Divine Mercy, which I had prayed many times. I especially loved the ending, "Jesus, I trust in You."

Something in that beautiful painting spoke to me. In the rays of mercy, I felt the beginning of a healing. I understood I needed to go to confession and confess about the vasectomy. It was only then that I realized how wrong it was; it was as if my blinders were removed. I waited to speak to a priest, and this wonderful man listened, consoled, and gave me things to think about. By God's grace, I was set free from the burden I had carried for many years. I was on a spiritual high! I finally felt alive in the Spirit, and I knew in my heart I was a new creation.

The retreat met a very specific need in our spiritual lives and in our married life. On the way home, Jeff shared that during his time of silence, prayer, and discussion with a priest, he too had felt the burden he carried about the decision to have a vasectomy lifted. As his wife, I had given my consent and was equally culpable. Interestingly, neither of us had discussed the guilt we carried for many years because we didn't want to cause a feeling of guilt or blame. We were mature enough, thankfully, that we each took our own personal responsibility, and I believe this was a gift from God. It would have been easy to point a finger or blame each other for the decision. I wish our confessions had been earlier, but first we needed to mature in our faith.

We never considered a vasectomy reversal. In fact, I didn't even know about this procedure until another one of my friends lamented about her husband's vasectomy. I was silent but fumed inside. Another one? I thought. Vasectomies seemed like an epidemic among married women, and the ones I knew were Christians! My friend opened her planner and showed me the phone number of a doctor who did reversals. Karen kept me apprised of her studies, and she located other doctors who also did reversals, but all charged enormous fees and were located out of state. She kept this number just in case her husband decided to have a reversal.

Karen impulsively took a sheet of paper, scribbled the doctor's name and number on it, and handed it to me. She was a fellow Catholic homeschool mom and one of the few people who knew about our situation. I had sworn her to secrecy. It seemed that for my generation, vasectomy was the new birth control. People were warned about the dangers of the birth control pill, so this seemed like a safer option, regardless of the moral consequences.

My friend grieved that she couldn't have more children and kept hoping that one day an affordable doctor would come along before she was too old to have more children. I didn't want to think about my mistake any longer. I was forgiven, and I wanted to get on with my life. Even so, I knew that if we wanted to, we could afford the surgery. I went home and shared about the discovery. My husband wasn't excited at the thought of another surgery. Yet that day, a small seed was planted.

 **Chapter 8**
Life with Kids

... from whom the whole body, joined and held together by every supporting ligament, with the proper functioning of each part, brings about the body's growth and builds itself up in love.

— Ephesians 4:16

Month Eight
Your baby is approximately twelve inches long and almost doubles in weight by the end of the month. The lungs are the last organs to be fully developed. He is preparing for birth, dropping lower, and the head should be down. You will feel less pushing and kicking as your little one runs out of room. You may have contractions off and on.

****

My Protestant homeschool friends were still actively seeking to convert me. I believe this was divine providence because it forced me to delve into the Scriptures and Church teachings and to study like never before. One of my friends, a Baptist minister, was often heard on the local Christian radio station. When he invited me to his church, I remember telling him I was an Italian Catholic and the Vatican was in Rome, so it was part of my heritage. My Italian roots never left me.

Two of my good friends were Evangelical Christians, and I asked more about their faith. They explained the gifts of the Holy Spirit and speaking in tongues. I was curious to learn more. One amazing godly friend, Chris, said matter-of-factly, "Felice, just kneel down beside your bed and ask the Lord for the gift of the Holy Spirit, and He'll give it to you."

That was the strangest thing I had ever heard—kneel and pray for an infilling of the gifts of the Holy Spirit? How bizarre was that? I talked to my husband about it, and he shrugged it off, agreeing it sounded strange; but he reminded me that with the Sacrament of Confirmation we had the gifts of the Holy Spirit. I believed he was right, but I wondered if God had more gifts to give.

1 Corinthians 12 speaks about the gifts of the Holy Spirit, and I was especially touched by verses 12:4–6: *There are different kinds of spiritual gifts but the same Spirit; there are different forms of service but the same Lord; there are different workings but the same God who produces all of them in everyone.* The chapter goes on to explain that all the gifts are produced by one and the same Spirit. He gives gifts to each person, just as He decides. I wanted all the gifts. I continued studying more about the differences in faith traditions.

While I had many wonderful, faith-filled conversations with my friends, our discussions often turned back to Mary; she was such a sticking point for my Protestant friends. How could they not love the person who said yes to the angel Gabriel, even knowing the possibility of being stoned for being pregnant and not married? I would explain that Catholics venerate Mary because God the Father sent the Son through this most humble woman, who said yes: *Mary said, "Behold, I am the handmaid of the Lord. May it be done to me according to your word." Then the angel departed from her* (Luke 1:38). She was to be called Blessed among all. *For he has looked upon his handmaid's lowliness; behold, from now on will all ages call me blessed* (Luke 1:48).

Luke 1:46–55 is called the Magnificat, which is also the name of an international ministry where I would later, some fifteen years in the future, volunteer for over ten years before I gave my testimony. Thank you, Lord, for working things out in my life.

It hit me during these conversations that if my friends were not protesting what they erroneously thought the Catholic Church taught, they would be Catholic! I was astounded that we had to agree to disagree on so few concepts because we totally agreed on the main concept: salvation is only through Christ. I loved my friends, but it was totally exhausting to continue to defend my beliefs. However, what I failed to realize was that God was stretching and teaching me.

I was learning wonderful things about my faith, and I was frustrated and sad that I didn't have more like-minded, Catholic homeschooling friends, so I prayed to God to bring me some. I didn't realize at that time that my Baptist friend Patti, at whose house we met at for coffee all those years ago, was attending local moms' groups at various churches to share the wonders of homeschooling. She went to a nearby Catholic moms' group, and they were so excited to learn about homeschooling. In fact, four of them wanted to learn more. I knew nothing about this meeting until years later. I feel this situation was orchestrated by God. He used my friend Patti to find Catholic friends for me! I'm so thankful for Patti; she felt homeschooling was ordained by God to raise godly children. It was her mission to share with as many who would listen. To this day, I love that lady!

Field trips were the way homeschoolers got together for socialization. One of the myths about homeschooling perpetuated by those who feared the ever-growing movement was that homeschooled children were unsocialized. Nothing was further from the truth. In fact, if we attended all the available field trips at the time, we'd never be home for the academic part of education.

Heading to a field trip on Sanibel Island, I followed a fifteen-passenger van covered with religious bumper stickers. I knew this had to be a homeschool family, and as I followed in my shiny BMW with the sunroof open and not one sticker, I rolled my eyes. Another one that would try to convert me! Upon arrival, I saw her talk to another mom, yet this one was wearing a cross with Jesus on it! Could she be a Catholic?

Cristina, who wore the cross, was sweet, had a Spanish accent, and asked me a ton of questions about homeschooling. Her children were little, and she was just beginning. Veronique, who drove the large van filled with children, also sported an accent—this one French. I knew I had found my soulmates: both ladies were as comfortable with their ethnicity as I was with mine, and both were Catholic! The Lord had sent me lifelong friends. Both are humble, godly women. They will dislike my saying this, but they are spiritual giants. I learned so much about faith and God through them.

One had nine children, and the other had four. God had brought me women who were open to life and having more children, who were Spirit-filled, and who had embraced the Baptism of the Holy Spirit as committed Catholic Christians. However, I didn't know this at the time. I continue to see the hand of the Lord as I look back. Sometime later, I happened to meet Cristina at the library. She had a stack of theological books, so I asked her what she was researching. She said, "I'm preparing to give a teaching. Why don't you come?" I didn't know how to politely say no, and if she was teaching on a religious topic that was Catholic, maybe I should attend. I dislike going anywhere by myself, and I tried very hard to get someone to go with me, but no one would. Either Jeff or I had to stay home to watch the children, and he opted to let me go since she was my friend.

I was surprised. This turned out to be a Life in the Spirit seminar, with in-depth teaching about the gifts of the Holy Spirit. These Catholic Christians were very boisterous; I was offered a tambourine, which I hastily turned down. Whatever had I gotten myself into? This was way out of my comfort zone. They were singing and praising God. Some had their eyes closed, and others' hands were raised upward. The songs were uplifting and happy but certainly not the normal church fare. If I could have left I would, but after all I had come to hear my friend's talk.

Once the teachings began, I was captivated; the talks were inspiring. When my friend Cristina spoke, I felt that she was anointed and the Lord was speaking words of wisdom through her meant specifically for me. The next day

I returned, and there was an offer for prayer—for a deeper infilling of the Holy Spirit! This was what my Evangelical friends talked about. Catholics were asking the Lord for a greater infilling of the Holy Spirit as well? I didn't have time to consider how the Lord had planted seeds in my heart, preparing me for this moment. All those years of prayer, study, and seeking Him beforehand had led to this. Even homeschooling my children, which allowed me to meet Christian friends who helped me search for a deeper understanding of the Bible, was a factor. God was touching my children's hearts, but He was touching mine as well, and I wanted more!

I was prayed for, and I received the gifts of the Holy Spirit! The lady who prayed for me asked me to sing in tongues; she said God wanted to give me something special. I thought she had to be kidding. No way was I speaking in tongues, let alone singing in tongues, in front of them. However, rather than singing I thought I could at least try to praise God, and it came out different than I planned. The next thing I knew, she was praising God and thanking Him for giving me the gift of tongues.

I had my prayer language! I was more joyous than ever before. I felt on fire with the Holy Spirit—ready to preach, teach, or do whatever the Lord wanted of me. It was a dedication to the God I had served off and on throughout my life, and I thought this was the culmination of all my years on earth. In the same way I felt created to teach, I now felt created to serve God in some capacity, and I couldn't wait to learn how He would have me do His work.

That day was our wedding anniversary, and my parents were keeping our children overnight at their house so Jeff and I could go out to dinner. I was so excited to recount my experiences of the Life in the Spirit seminar that at one point Jeff asked me to keep my voice down. Our intimate private dinner turned out a bit differently than he expected. He wasn't quite sure what to make of it, but he was genuinely happy. I am married to the most incredible man—the one that God specifically chose for me. He has been steady through all our ups and downs. Even a Spirit-filled wife didn't deter his love.

Afterward, we both enrolled in a Bible study at the home of Cristina and Bob, and we studied the book of Corinthians. It was all about the gifts of the Spirit. Jeff later attended a Life in the Spirit seminar, at their invitation. It was my turn to stay home with our kids, and he was blessed by the experience.

Along with many people from our Bible study, we began attending a weekly Charismatic prayer group. It was a wonderful time of praying, sharing, and seeing miracles and healings take place. We witnessed physical as well as spiritual healing, but most of the time we sang praises to God, prayed, and listened to uplifting teachings. We watched as God the Father, Jesus the Son, and the Holy Spirit touched the lives of those who attended.

One of those healings was for my husband. After a Bible study, Bob, an orthopedic surgeon, asked if anyone wanted prayer. Bob was an anomaly to me. I remember telling him when I realized he had the gift of healing, "Doctor, if you pray for the healing of your patients, you will work yourself out of a job!" I was half teasing, but he said God was the healer, and his part was to pray. He noticed that Jeff was uncomfortable and asked him if he had back pain. Jeff said it was minor but chronic. He had this pain since he was a college athlete. The doctor asked if he wanted prayers, and he shrugged his shoulders and said, "Sure." He looked at me as if to say, "What did I get myself into?"

The doctor asked him to sit all the way back in the chair and extend his legs and said, "One of your legs is a bit longer than the other, which is perfectly normal—but we are going to pray that it grows to equal the other." I was shocked! Growing a leg—didn't anyone else think this was abnormal? As he was explaining what he was going to pray for, people were gathering around Jeff, extending their hands and praying in tongues. The doctor asked if someone wanted to watch to see when the leg grew and to alert everyone when it did. I volunteered, amazed that no one else wanted to witness this phenomenon.

Of course, I didn't believe this would happen, but why not watch? What could it hurt? I had prayed with the others many times for miracles and witnessed healings, but nothing like this! Thoughts came back to me about faith as small as a mustard seed—the lessons from the Bible taught by my grandmother. Did I have faith as small as a mustard seed? I believed my faith was so much bigger, yet I was still hesitant. I didn't want to test God like I had as a child. If God chose to heal, fine; if not, that was fine as well.

Well, it happened!

I watched my husband's leg grow to equal the other, and I shouted out that it grew! Those praying took this information as a sign to begin thanking and praising God. Alleluia! I began to praise God as well, especially when Bob asked Jeff to stand. His chronic pain was gone. This started another round of praise and alleluias to God.

Bob launched into a lengthy and detailed explanation about ways that Satan tries to rob us of our faith. One way, he explained, could be the return of the back pain, or pain in a different spot or with different intensity. If this happened, he said, we were to come against the enemy's attack, and he taught us how to pray. We were to bind the pain, in the precious name of Jesus—rebuke it, sending it to the foot of the cross for Jesus to take care of—and continue to pray.

This was a huge faith-building event for me. As a child, I did not see a mountain move, but here I watched my husband's leg grow before my very eyes with no expectant faith that it would happen! God's ways are not ours. I can't imagine His unlimited love for me which he has shown in the ways He has stepped into my life when I most needed Him. Even with all the times of prayers answered that I didn't even ask for, this was beyond anything I could hope for. Being an eyewitness with a front row seat to a miracle for the love of my life was an even greater gift. I was ready to take on the world and begin praying for everyone's healing!

The next day we took our children to the beach. While we were there, Jeff was trying to read the newspaper. He was seated on a blanket on the hard ground and was moving around in discomfort. I asked him what was wrong. He dismissed it as nothing—only a pain in his back, but in a different place. He told me it was minor, and he was accustomed to back pain. I wasn't about to let this opportunity pass me by, so I reminded him about the instruction we had received the night before about rebuking Satan. I assured him I was going to pray for him, right there and then on Fort Myers Beach. I didn't give him much of a choice; in fact, he didn't have time to put the paper away. I quickly prayed, and God took his pain away. He no longer has this back pain, and he has stopped sleeping with a pillow under his leg. I praise God—He is faithful!

At the invitation of our prayer group leaders, Jeff and I attended the regional Catholic Charismatic Conference and had no idea what to expect. Even though we attended prayer meetings, we were a little on the reserved side to say the least. We sat as far to the back as we could. The leaders of our prayer group were sitting way up front near the blaring speakers, and Cristina kept coming back to check on us to see if we were okay. I guess she was concerned because we looked like we were out of our comfort zone. If I thought our small group gatherings were on fire with praises to the Lord, that was the junior high group compared to the graduate-school version we were now witnessing. I was overwhelmed with the praising of Jesus by joyous people surrounding me.

Our teachings from prayer group and Scripture study had prepared us intellectually for the fact that some people are slain in the Spirit, and we soon learned that at the end of the evening service, there would be an anointing for those who chose to go forward for a blessing. It was explained as a blessing and prayer for a deeper infilling of the Holy Spirit—we could rest in the Spirit and receive anointing from God, but it was optional. My husband was determined that if anyone was going to pray for him, it would have to be a Catholic priest, and he led me to the line where the priest was praying. As we neared the front of the line we witnessed a resting in the Spirit. The infilling of the Holy Spirit is so strong and powerful that in yielding, the Spirit can bring us divine consolation and spiritual blessings. Sometimes people can't remain standing—the power of the Holy Spirit is so overwhelming.

Both Jeff and I were very nervous but open to more blessings! It wasn't something either of us was particularly seeking, and we were both determined to stand throughout the blessing. When we finally arrived up front, I was prayed for by the kind priest, and then I smiled and walked away. When I turned to see if Jeff was following me, I saw that as the priest's hands got closer to him, his body moved back—not his feet, just his upper torso. I can only describe it as a magnet with a repelling effect. Finally, as if tiring, the priest gestured a blessing from a distance and down my husband went! I stood there in tears. I couldn't believe it. The priest had not even touched him. My husband was a bit disoriented because he tried to rise to his feet too quickly. Later we learned that if you rest in the Spirit, you should yield to the blessing of the Spirit and get up carefully or you might be dizzy.

A Scripture verse that helped us was 2 Chronicles 5:14: *. . . the priests could not stand to minister because of the cloud, for the glory of the LORD filled the house of God* (New American Standard Bible, emphasis added).

Another helpful passage was John 18: 4–6: Jesus, knowing everything that was going to happen to him, went out and said to them, *"Whom are you looking for?" They answered him, "Jesus the Nazorean." He said to them, "I AM." Judas his betrayer was also with them. When he said to them, "I AM," they turned away and fell to the ground* (emphasis added).

Jeff and I were renewed in our faith. I cannot tell you what a gift the Lord gave me to have a husband that was my partner in life and faith. It was a joy to experience these things together. I had been studying the faith by way of apologetics for years, but now I was experiencing all the gifts of the Holy Spirit with my husband.

The children were older now and stayed at home when we went to prayer meetings. I arranged our schedules so that we had prayer time in the morning. They soon learned that if they interrupted my prayer time for something unnecessary, I wasn't much fun the rest of the day. If they allowed me this time, I was much happier and joyful. Kids learn quickly.

I was giving and renewing my life to God. He had become so real—the focus and center of my life. I was journaling and praying the Bible with renewed fervor. I asked the Lord for a prophetic word. I had heard many people in my prayer group utter prophetic words and have them confirmed with a Bible verse from someone else or another word that perfectly coincided. I was extremely aware of the risk of being deceived by the enemy, so I would test everything I thought I was receiving from the Lord. I would say things like "If this thought isn't from Jesus Christ who walked the ground in Nazareth and is the true Son of God, be gone!" Still, the thought would linger, but I didn't trust that I could ever be worthy enough to hear a prophetic word from God.

However, on my birthday I was sitting in my room with my Bible and journal, and I reasoned with the Lord. I told Him that it was my birthday (as if He didn't know) and all I wanted was a prophetic word. Then, I closed my eyes and waited.

The first thing I heard in my mind was Psalms 46:10: *Be still and know that I am God.* I received the most beautiful words as I waited, and hurried to write them down so I would not forget. I was elated, but just to be sure I decided to ask our prayer group leader for confirmation. She would always tell us that nice words are just that, but we should have some biblical confirmation or learn that someone else was getting the same or similar words in their prayers. If not, it wasn't from God. I was fearful I would utter something false, so I said nothing in our gatherings.

One More Child

When she looked at the words I wrote, she shook her head in affirmation and said, "Yes, it looks like it is authentic," handed back my journal, and walked away. This was the confirmation that I needed that indeed I could pray and hear a beautiful prophecy from God. My friend Cristina, who was standing nearby, told me later that she was shocked at the affirmation because it was rarely given. Yet I knew in my heart that I had heard the Lord, and that was enough for me. Yet another layer of the onion peel of my life was turned back, and I was ready to study and go deeper in my faith.

Chapter 9
Unexpected Blessings

Your eyes saw me unformed; in your book all are written down; my days were shaped, before one came to be.

— Psalm 139:16

Month Nine

Your baby will put on weight every week. This will help sustain him the first few days of life. His brain is growing rapidly. The protective hair and skin are being shed, and the lungs are finishing their development. Any day, a new baby will be born.

****

On the outside I was self-confident. I tackled any job, and I never felt there was anything, I couldn't do, but inside I was still concerned about my secret. Yes, I was forgiven, and that's all some people need. For me it was not enough. I couldn't stop thinking about it and wondered how I would approach my husband with the idea of a reversal. I so wanted to be in God's will in every way possible.

I approached my husband about the reversal. This was the first time that our marriage was on rocky grounds because we rarely fought about anything, and this was a topic he didn't want to discuss. True to form, he quickly agreed this would be a good idea but not now. Jeff likes to think about things. He doesn't make snap decisions like I do—he says he is the string to my kite. This has worked out wonderfully because otherwise I'd be in the stratosphere. My crazy ideas are bounced off him first, and he is the best listener in the world. His instincts are good, and he has warned me off various projects and has been right.

Even so, allowing him time to think was not in my playbook, especially since I had thought about this for some time. There were several heated discussions and serious making up, but nothing happened to change his mind. I released him to the Lord and said, "If it is Your will, Lord, you deal with him." One day Jeff approached me and revealed that he had indeed been thinking about the reversal. He said, "In life, when we sin, we can't often go back and change the wrong. In this case we can correct it—and I've decided I'm ready."

Finally, we both felt free and excited. It wasn't necessarily that we wanted our family size to increase; we were content as we were. We just wanted to be open to one more child—if that was the Lord's plan. Homeschooling Neal turned out better than expected. He was well adjusted, learning, and making progress each year. There were some limitations to his abilities, but we were sure Neal would be self-sufficient and not a burden on the extended family in the future. Christina flourished in the homeschool setting. She was smart and kept me on my toes. She was argumentative, with air-tight reasoning, and I seriously thought she had a career in law someday. Ever the social butterfly, she made friends no matter what their age and easily fell into leadership roles.

The reversal wasn't smooth sailing; it took two separate trips to the doctor and a year of waiting before the procedure was performed. Jeff changed his mind after the first doctor visit. I have no idea what the doctor told him, and he no longer remembers. However, he decided to wait almost another year after the first visit. Finally, the procedure was completed, and it was a success with no complications. This decision to go through with the reversal was the best thing for our marriage. We were closer than ever; it was as if an invisible barrier had been removed.

The idea that we could have more children was always in the back of our mind, and I can't put into words how that made a difference. Our children were thirteen and eleven, and I regretted that we had waited so long and I was so old. I didn't think we'd be able to have more children, but I was open to one more.

However, I soon found myself expecting a baby! I was joyous and sick at the same time. I had not experienced morning sickness with my first two, but this time I was often sick in the evening as well. During my pregnancy, we homeschooled in a relaxed style that suited both of my children; there was still lots of reading aloud and hands-on projects. The previous year I had begun speaking and writing and had launched a publishing company called Media Angels. Anyone looking at my life from the outside would consider this bad timing. Yet God's timing is always perfect—and I was still learning this life lesson.

At times I felt overwhelmed and out of control, especially before Christmas. School work had to be wrapped up for break, and the big Christmas Eve family celebration for the birthdays of Neal and Christina was fast approaching, not to mention Christmas Day. In addition, my publishing company was planning upcoming speaking and writing projects. I felt so behind.

One day I was waiting to pick up the kids from Christmas pageant practice at the parish center at church. I felt like I was going to be sick and was looking for the nearest restroom. A beautiful lady approached me with a baby in her arms. She excitedly congratulated me on my pregnancy; she was literally gushing. I didn't know her, and I didn't want to talk to her, so I turned to sarcasm: "Yes. Thank you. I'm pregnant and in my Elizabethan years." This was a reference to the advanced age of Elizabeth when she had John the Baptist. She looked at me keenly and asked my age. I told her I was thirty-eight, but I'd have this baby soon after I turned thirty-nine. She explained that the precious baby in her arms was her fourth, and she had tried and failed to have children for the first twenty years of her married life. She was forty-four years old and in her prime. I congratulated her, and we went on to become friends for the short time she lived in my town.

I believe these are divine appointments. The Lord sent this lady to me to say, "You'll be fine and I'm in control." God also has a sense of humor, and I believe he added, "If you think you are old now, wait until you see how old you

One More Child

will be with your last child." God does have a perfect plan even for apparently random conversations. I had my fourth child at forty-two and my fifth child at forty-four—the same age as this lady.

This was a new chapter in my life. I had finally embraced *Humanae Vitae*. I was open to God's will in my life. I had dedicated my life to God so many times over the course of my life, but now, at last, I truly meant the words in Scripture attributed to the Blessed Mother: *Mary said, "Behold, I am the handmaid of the Lord. May it be done to me according to your word."* (Luke 1:38 emphasis added).

Giving God my heart without giving Him all of me, my marriage, my children, my openness to more children was not truly giving all. How could I follow Him in every sense of the word *follow* while continuing to pick and choose how I wanted to follow Him?

My rationale as an immature Christian had been, "You can have my life, Lord, but I don't want to give You any authority over the number of children I wish to have. It is my decision. It is my body. It is my life. I am in charge because You gave me free will to decide." While I didn't say this outright, it was how I secretly felt—and how I had lived my life, until the reversal.

I know I am not alone. Many well-meaning Christians have done the same thing. I knew them and loved them as sisters in Christ. They loved God and lived their lives in a way that was pleasing, except this one area—the area of birth control. However, keeping any aspect of our lives from God's control is sinful, regardless of free will.

Another random conversation included a friend who said her daughter was told by God in prayer that they should not have any more children, so they decided on a surgical option. My first thought was, "If God truly does not want you to have children, or any more children, and you are open to His will—you won't have any more children. Why would you need to take it into your own hands or do something permanently?"

We tell ourselves what we want to hear. We compartmentalize our decisions. Often they are in the deep recesses of our minds, far away from conscious thought, but never too far away from God. He sees through our walls and those tiny, dark places where we don't give Him permission to go. He allows us by our own free will to do as we please, but I couldn't be totally free until I gave Him permission to be Lord over all aspects of my life.

I have been in great health in my "Elizabethan years," praise be to God. Having young children in my later years curtailed many of my activities like being a CCD teacher, attending the weekly Charismatic prayer group meetings, date nights with my husband, and other activities I enjoyed. However, these times of curtailed activities now seem like they were short lived.

All of our children—both the Christmas Eve babies born in my younger years, Neal and Christina, and those born in my older years, Nick, Anne, and Mike—have been such a blessing. I cannot imagine my life without any of my children. They have impacted my husband and me personally as well as many people throughout the years. To think the last three children would not be here unless we took that leap of faith and had the vasectomy reversal makes me shudder.

While I was in the process of praying about whether I could tell my story or not, I realized I had to tell my children the truth. Jeff and I had kept them in the dark. To us it had been a secret—a horrible decision we had made that was against God's natural law. Our children now needed to learn that their parents were fallible and that if it was not for a vasectomy reversal they would not have been born. You can imagine how stunned they were after that conversation!

The outcome is the knowledge that God has something special planned for their lives. There is some reason He wanted them born. Yes, God has special plans for all of us—but I like to think there are amazing blessings in store for the children who are born due to reversals. What the children do with this information as they age is up to them, but the seeds are planted.

The fact that there was a large age gap between my two oldest children and my next child brought up many questions from friends or strangers. People often asked me my age, which is humbling, especially when I already felt old. One lady said, "Well I'm only thirty-five and I have not had any children yet, so this gives me hope!" I was a silent witness without realizing the impact. All the glory goes to God.

As I shared my story within our homeschool community, friends who were considering a vasectomy or a reversal would ask to talk to both my husband and me. I lost count of the number of families that had reversals not only because of our story but also because of being open to listening to God's will for their lives. The first opportunity I had to publicly share my testimony about the amazing healing power of God was at the invitation of the leadership of the Magnificat Prayer Breakfast, where I was asked to speak soon after saying yes to the Lord about writing this book. Being open to more children has brought our family joy and peace. It is a blessing beyond anything I can imagine.

Love is a very strong attraction, and we love our children. Can you imagine not having the children you love in your family because of a choice? A decision you make willingly? I know it is not popular to speak out against birth control, against sterilization, and against vasectomies, but I know that many Christian women who know, love, and want to serve the Lord have fallen prey to lies, just as I did. They are willingly saying no to the children that could be part of their lives. They are saying, "No, thank you, Lord. I have enough." I've often thought that the enemy doesn't want the world populated with Christian kids who love God. Now that my eyes are open, I look back and I see what I call a Christian blindness. I was clearly duped.

The doctor who did Jeff's reversal still has a huge billboard on the interstate that has a new message: the cost of child support is approximately $600 a month, and the cost of a vasectomy is $600 one time. It is cheaper to stop having children. This is the world in which we live. Not surprisingly in this age of promiscuous sex and birth control, the sign is considered humorous. A business friend laughingly told me about the sign, and I used this an opportunity to share that my youngest three are the result of that doctor's magnificent work in reversals. Once God allowed me the grace to tell my story, it keeps coming up again and again.

Humanae Vitae accurately predicted the state of our world. Women and men are not cherished as unique individuals but look upon one another's bodies as merely objects to be used for pleasure. I often wish I had the courage to make an appointment and walk in to this doctor's office with my three youngest children and thank him for the reversal! Instead, I pray for him daily. The random seed my mother planted by giving me *Humanae Vitae* as a newlywed eventually took root many years later.

Recently, I was helping my youngest son pack for his freshman year of college, out of state. I picked up his copy of *The Diary of Sister Faustina*—one of my mother's favorite books that I had given a copy of to each child. I opened it randomly and was surprised to see that the date of the first journal entry was the same day that my mother died (in a different year, of course). Nothing is random with God.

My father was lost after my mother's death in 1999, so when Christina graduated from college and was married, my husband invited my father to move in with us. The three youngest children had the experience of living with a grandparent just like I did. Although my father was vocal in his opinions on family events and my parenting, I was not surprised. The children learned what it meant to age with grace, to be cared for, and to care for others. Overall, it was a blessing. He died on the feast day of St. Joseph, the foster father of Jesus. That was his favorite saint and holiday. Again, there are no random coincidences for God.

I was praying and thanking God for this gift—these seemingly random dates that meant so much to my parents. How special that the Lord allows this for those He loves! I felt in my heart the Lord saying that my parents are with Him and that these dates were not for those who have passed but for those who are living. They are small signs of God's providence for us—His care in the minutiae of our lives. I praise God that He gives me eyes that see.

I don't look for signs and wonders as I believe that God's work is complete and all we need to know is taught in Scripture and tradition—the Holy Bible and our Church.

However, we can learn so much about His love for us by being aware and open to listening to His small, still voice.

People say that ignorance is bliss—but it isn't. It's considered a sin of omission. Look it up. Ignorance causes heartache, guilt, and lifelong pain that only prayer and true forgiveness can heal. I want to encourage you that freedom from sin is truly life in God. Only God could set me free, and He wants to do the same for you.

I feel especially blessed that the Lord opened my eyes. As you can see, it was a long process. I am impatient, and this world encourages impatience through fast food, instant information on the Internet, and contact with people all over the world via social media. Yet my children forced me to slow down, set my priorities in the right order, and follow through on promises, which made me focus on what is important in life.

I pray that the Lord leads you to a life-changing decision, whatever that happens to be in your life. If you feel challenged, take it to the Lord. Ask Him if you never have before. Grow closer to God and petition Him. You may be surprised to learn that it is never too late! It is never too late to turn back to God. The true God, not some New Age counterfeit, is waiting there for you, with open arms.

I now live my life with God at the center. All projects moving forward will involve Christian ministry as He opens doors. I believe that if we give our hearts to God—if we want Him to be an integral part of our lives and want to follow Him in all things and in all ways—it can only be on His terms, not ours. When I recommitted my life to God, everything became clear. I truly want to serve God in all things, and I ask Him to lead me and allow me to share His love with others. I pray He does the same in your life.

About the Author:

Felice Gerwitz has been married to her best friend, Jeff, for over 38 years, is the mother of five children, and has eight grandchildren. She is an author, podcaster, and the owner of Media Angels, Inc.

When she is not writing or podcasting, Felice can be found in the kitchen baking, making crafts with her grandchildren, or at a field, watching a softball or baseball game. The Gerwitz family lives in Florida.

If you would like to contact Felice, send an email to felice@mediaangels.com or visit her website: https://www.MediaAngels.com.

www.ingramcontent.com/pod-product-compliance
Lightning Source LLC
Chambersburg PA
CBHW070523030426
42337CB00016B/2087